# Your Mind

Dr Peter Toon
Penny Tripp
Mark Evans

Published1990 by
Harrap Publishing Group Ltd
Chelsea House
26 Market Square
Bromley
Kent BR1 1NA
By arrangement with Amanuensis Books Ltd

ISBN 0 245-60008-6

This book was designed and produced by
Amanuensis Books Ltd
12 Station Road
Didcot
Oxfordshire OX11 7LL
UK

Editorial and art director: Loraine Fergusson
Senior editor: Lynne Gregory
Authenticator: Dr Hugh Pelly
Illustration:  Loraine Fergusson, Ron Freeborn, David Gifford, Lynne
Gregory, Marian Whiting
Charts: Mick Brennan, Loraine Fergusson
Cover design: Roger King Graphic Studios

MGI Prime Health, the health division of Municipal General Insurance Ltd,
part of the Municipal Insurance Group, has contributed to the cost of this
publication.

The information contained in this book has been obtained from professional
medical sources and every care has been taken to ensure that it is consistent with
current medical practice. However,  it is intended only as a guide to current
medical practice and not as a substitute for the advice of your medical practitioner
which must, on all occasions, be taken.

# Contents

# Your brain

Your brain's primary function is to protect you from harm and ensure that everything in your body is working as it should do. In order to achieve this, it has to know what is going on inside your body, on the surface of your body, and in the environment that surrounds you. It is at the heart of your body's communications systems, collecting information from inside it via internal receptors and from outside it by means of specialized sensory organs, storing that information in its (i.e. your) memory, communicating between all parts of your body, and triggering off actions designed to ensure survival.

Because the brain has a limitless storage capacity, your present actions (whether conscious or unconscious, or connected with physical or mental functions) are usually based on what happened in the past when you or your body's systems were faced with similar circumstances.This, in effect, is what is meant by 'memory', and means that you and your systems do not have to react to everything you experience as though it were completely new. It is thought that long-term memory is assured when physical changes occur in your brain and actually imprint a particular behavior pattern on your tissues. Memory, whether you are consciously aware of it or not. is therefore a short-cut to efficient action.

You are an immensely complex organism, and survival depends on the body's ability to register and compensate for changes in both the internal and external environments. Your delicately-balanced life-support systems depend for their health on particular conditions and, if you were unable to adapt to even slight changes in those conditions, you would not survive. For example if you, like a fly, were so dependent on a stable air temperature that you would die if it fluctuated more than a couple of degrees, you would not last long. The brain, however, can register such a change and initiate action designed to maintain body temperature no matter what the air temperature might be.

The brain is therefore responsible for maintaining your body in a state called homeostasis, in which it can sustain all the chemical processes which contribute to keeping you alive. Its capacity for receiving, storing and acting on information, however, would not in itself be enough to ensure homeostasis unless it could also coordinate all your systems so that they work together rather than against each other.

All your life-support systems are closely linked, and dependent on each other. You could not digest and use food, for example, without a circulatory system that absorbed and distributed nutrients around the body.

You would not even be able to get your food as far as your mouth in the first place were it not for the fact that you could register the presence of something to eat, then precisely and accurately, use your hands (and, possibly, tools as well) to put it there. Without even having to think about it, you open your mouth, start chewing, begin to produce saliva then, again, without conscious thought, embark on the complex sequence of actions involved in swallowing.

It is the brain, then, that ensures that all these actions start happening at just the right moment. The result is that you make no unnecessary movements, and your body starts producing enzymes (the chemicals that help you digest your food) only when they are needed. If all these activities were uncoordinated, food might pass right through your digestive system without being broken down into a form the body could use, even if it managed to get into the right place to begin with.

The brain would not be able to perform its coordinating role were it not in touch with every single part of the body, as well as with the outside world. Hence the special sensory organs, those concerned with sight, hearing, smell and taste, which react to stimuli (messages) from outside, and the internal receptors which gather information relating to things like temperature, touch and body position (see pages 14-23).

Once the significance of the information has been established, there also has to be a way of initiating any necessary responses to it, again, some kind of connection between the central processing unit and the organs responsible for action. Your brain is linked with its

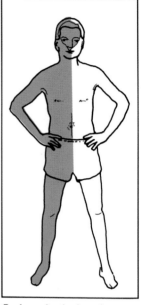

**Brain and spinal cord**
*The most sophisticated sensors would be useless if they were not connected to a central point where their information could be registered, interpreted and used. The right-hand side of the brain is responsible for the left-hand side of the body, and vice versa.*

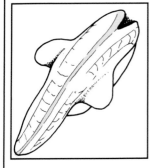

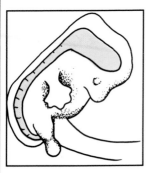

**Development**
*Your brain began to develop only days after you were conceived, long before your mother even knew she was pregnant. At that time, what was to become your brain was simply the top end of your spinal cord, made of the same kind of nervous tissue. This tissue, central gray matter consisting of the bodies of nerve cells, overlaid by white matter made up of nerve fibers, is found throughout the nervous system.*

information-gatherers, and with its action-producing systems, in two ways: one via a high-speed communications network called your nervous system, and one based on hormones (the endocrine system) which works more slowly. Both nervous and endocrine systems are important in maintaining homeostasis.

The brain, however, is more than just an ultra-sophisticated computer, the hub of a complex communications system. If this were all it was, human beings would be no more than robots which, programmed to behave in particular ways, would have no choice but to react to given circumstances in a predetermined fashion. Instead, the brain makes you an individual, unique and distinct from everybody else.

The brain is not just responsible for coordinating and controlling all the activities that go on in your body all the time, which are essential for your survival, but of which you are largely unaware. It is also where the 'higher' functions that make you human originate: your ability to think, for example, or to choose between one course of action and another. Your capacity to perform these functions, and your ability to use language, to judge and to plan, to reason and to learn, to feel, to be creative and appreciate the creativity of others, is also something for which your brain is responsible.

Scientists suspect that everything that goes on in your brain, even the fact that you like this piece of music better than that one, may well turn out to be the result of specific electro-chemical events that happen there, but at the moment they accept that they do not know. Although they have identified certain areas of the brain which appear to be responsible for certain functions, they admit that they are not entirely sure how everything actually works.

## Gray and white matter

Nerve cells, or neurones, are the basic units of your nervous system. Their shape and size depends on where they are and what they are designed to do, but they all have the same basic structure: a large central nucleus

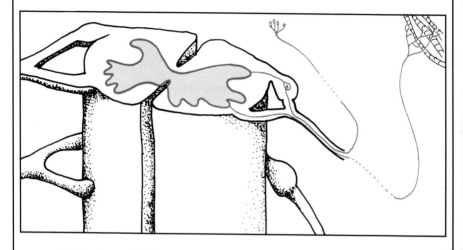

surrounded by the cell body, from which nerve fibers extend. Nerve fibers are responsible for bringing in stimuli (messages) to the cell body, passing them to other neurones, or taking them away from the cell body. Neurones are thus of three basic types: sensory neurones (those which bring the stimulus in from a sense organ or internal receptor), connector (or association) neurones which sort out information in your brain and spinal cord, and motor neurones which relay messages back out to your body and which initiate some kind of action.

You will find more information on how messages are actually transmitted throughout your nervous system on page 23.

As you grew in the womb, the top end of your spinal cord gradually swelled to form three primitive brain regions: the fore-, mid- and hind-brain. By the time you were born, the areas you would be using most in your adult life had become thicker and more developed: the fore-brain had grown the most to form the two hemispheres of your cerebrum, while the mid-brain had developed into an internal structure concerned with interpreting what you see. The front part of your hind-brain had become your cerebellum, and its rearmost parts had developed into the medulla of the mature brain stem.

*One of the simplest nerve connections is the 'reflex arc'. A sensation registered in the nerve endings of the skin causes impulses to rush up the sensory fibers within the spinal nerve and travel through the gray matter in the center of the spinal cord to stimulate the motor fibers which cause the muscles to contract. The impulse never reaches the brain. This reduces the time between feeling a sensation and responding to it, vital if the body needs to remove part of itself swiftly from danger, e.g. from a hot surface. This reflex is what the doctor is testing when doing a knee jerk.*

# The adult brain

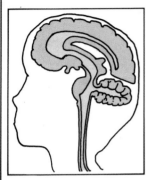

*Deep within the cerebrum are ventricles, cavities containing the protective, nourishing cerebrospinal fluid. All the fluid-filled ventricles inside your brain link up with a central canal that runs the length of your spinal cord.*

The adult brain weighs about 1.5 kilograms (3 pounds), looks like a shelled walnut and has the consistency of a ripe avocado. It contains about fifteen thousand million brain cells, grouped into sensory, motor and association centers (see below). It is protected from external damage by your bony skull, and by three layers of membranes called the meninges.

Between the layers of the meninges flows cerebrospinal fluid which acts as a liquid shock-absorber and washes out waste products. It also contains the oxygen and nourishment essential for the proper functioning of your nervous tissues. The same fluid protects, supports and nourishes your spinal cord, which together with your brain makes up your central nervous system.

## The cerebrum

This is the biggest part of your brain, and occupies most of your skull. It lies over the smaller cerebellum at the rear. The two halves (cerebral hemispheres) of your cerebrum are joined by the pons (meaning bridge) of white nervous tissue containing nerve fibers which aid communication between the two hemispheres.

The white matter which makes up the inner part of your cerebrum is covered by gray matter (containing nerve cell bodies) called the cerebral cortex. This is deeply folded to increase its area and the number of cell bodies it can house.

The whole cerebrum is divided into lobes, whose names (frontal, parietal, temporal and occipital) correspond to the skull bones that protect them.

Within the white matter of your cerebral hemispheres are clumps of gray matter, the cerebral nuclei. These are masses of nerve cell bodies which are connected to other parts of the brain. Damage to these areas leads to either uncontrollable muscle actions or paralysis.

### Function

The two halves of your cerebrum are not identical. They specialize in different things, but they are united and their

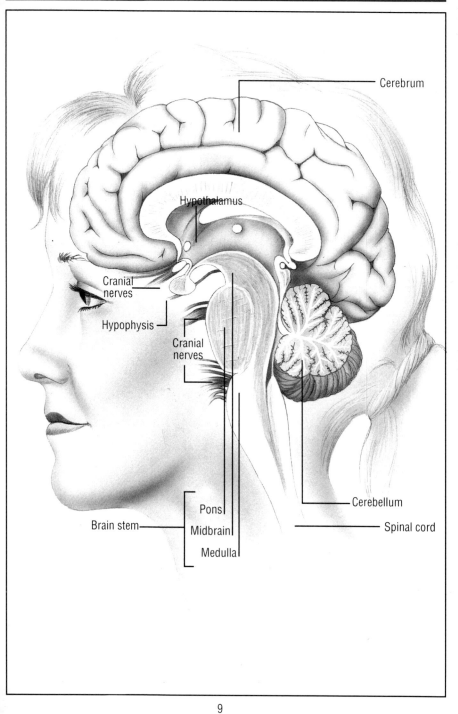

Cerebrum

Hypothalamus

Cranial
nerves

Hypophysis

Cranial
nerves

Cerebellum

Pons

Brain stem

Midbrain

Spinal cord

Medulla

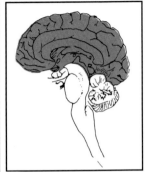

*The cerebrum*

abilities are complementary. The memory stored in each appears to be accessible to the other, so damage to one part of one hemisphere does not necessarily mean that a particular function will be lost. This can happen, however, when some functions, like your capacity for speech or writing, located in whichever of your hemispheres is dominant (see below), do not seem to be duplicated in the non-dominant, or minor, hemisphere.

The dominant hemisphere is usually the left one (associated with right-handedness, because the two hemispheres control functions in the opposite part of the body). The right hemisphere is dominant in left-handed people.

The cerebrum is responsible for many complex functions, and it has been possible to identify specific areas in it which control them.

Motor activities, such as muscle movements, are controlled by the nerve centers within the cortex near the front part of your cerebrum. Certain areas of the cerebral cortex control certain groups of muscles, so brain damage in these motor areas may result in paralysis of the muscles associated with them.

Sensory activities, such as sight, hearing and touch, are functions of the sensory areas of your cerebral cortex, which give you information that has been picked up by your sense organs. You know where your arms are, for example, because proprioceptors (sense organs) in your arm muscles send this information to your cerebral cortex. Without the sensory areas of the cerebrum, you would not know what objects felt like, how heavy they were, whether they were hot or cold; you would not hear sounds, or see light. There are motor and sensory areas in both your cerebral hemispheres.

Your memories, judgements, emotions and intelligence have their origins in the large association areas located to the side and in the front of your cerebral cortex. Other non-physical attributes - conscience and imagination, for example - are also associated with these areas.

Association areas are collections of nerve fibers

that link up motor and sensory areas, and make it possible for you to associate incoming sensations with past experience so that you can react appropriately. Your cerebral cortex is therefore that part of your brain which calculates the best course of action, that is, the one with the greatest immediate or long-term survival value, from all the sensory information and memory available to it. It then sends out appropriate 'action' commands.

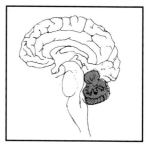

The cerebellum

It is the presence of association areas that makes human beings different from robots: you can behave in different ways depending on what is right for a particular situation. A robot does not have the capacity for making that kind of choice.

The cerebral cortex starts life as a blank slate, unlike other areas of your brain which are thought to contain built-in nerve circuits which maintain things like your heartbeat and blood pressure. The cortex does, however, have the potential to establish millions of incredibly complex connections which govern your responses to all sorts of stimuli, and it is these connections which form as a result of all the learning that takes place over a lifetime.

## The cerebellum

This part of your brain, sometimes called the 'little brain', lies underneath the occipital lobe of your cerebrum. Like the cerebrum, it consists of an outer, convoluted (folded) layer of gray matter over an inner core of white matter. Deep within the white matter are the gray areas of cerebral nuclei. Again, there are two hemispheres, this time joined by a mid-portion called the vermis.

### Functions

While your cerebral hemispheres are those parts of your brain mainly concerned with activities of which you are conscious, your cerebellum's functions are mostly related to control over posture, balance, and finely coordinated patterns of muscular movements.

The white matter of your cerebellum contains tracts (bundles) of nerve fibers. These carry sensory

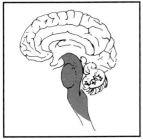

*The brain stem*

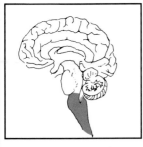

*The medulla oblongata is the lowest part of your brain and is, in effect, that part of the spinal cord which actually passes through the base of your skull. It consists of white matter, and is a major highway for nerve tracts on their way to and from the brain. It is here that these bundles of nerves cross over from left to right so that information to and from one side of the body is passed to the opposite side of the brain. This is why damage to one side of the brain affects activity on the other side of the body.*

impulses (messages) to your cerebellum from your muscles and the organs of balance contained in your ears, and may either come direct or via association centers elsewhere in your brain. Outgoing nerve fibers do not go directly to those organs which will eventually respond to an instruction to perform some kind of action; again, they travel via association centers so that activity can be carefully, but without your conscious intervention, coordinated.

Were it not for the cerebellum, your movements would be jerky, violent and spasmodic rather than smooth and controlled. Your cerebral cortex would be commanding a specific activity, but be unable to control its detailed execution. If your cerebellum is damaged, the information coming from proprioceptors in your muscles cannot be properly coordinated.

## The brain stem

Your brain stem connects the higher centers of your brain with your spinal cord. Its main parts are the medulla oblongata, the pons, the mid-brain, the thalamus and the hypothalamus.

### The medulla oblongata

Within the medulla's white matter are areas of gray matter, nerve cell bodies belonging to four of the cranial nerves which control conscious activities in the structures and organs of your shoulders, neck and head.

Other collections of gray matter within the medulla are the sites of what are called your vital or reflex centers. The cardiac center regulates heart beat, the vasoconstrictor center, the diameter of blood vessels. The respiratory center controls the rate and depth of breathing, and various visceral centers govern activities like swallowing and vomiting as well as the movements of your stomach and the secretion of digestive juices. All kinds of involuntary, reflex actions originate here.

### Mid-brain

This part of your brain connects the pons and cerebellum

below to the cerebrum above. It resembles the medulla and pons because it too contains bundles of nerve fibers going down from the brain to the spinal cord, and up towards the cerebral cortex. Two cranial nerves have their origins here, and four bumps called the corpora quadrigemina contain the centers that coordinate hearing and seeing. It is this part of your brain, for example, that allows you to locate the direction from which a particular sound is coming.

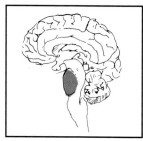

## The thalamus

Just above the mid-brain is an area of gray matter surrounded by white matter. This is the thalamus, a major relay center. Impulses entering your brain, from its own lower areas or your spinal cord, are processed here before being sent on to the cerebral cortex.

## The hypothalamus

Just below the thalamus is this vital area which works closely with the pituitary gland (see below) in order to maintain homeostasis (the constant internal environment necessary for your survival).

    The hypothalamus ensures that body temperature is kept normal, because it is sensitive to any fluctuations that may occur. It regulates food intake by being sensitive to hunger pains. A thirst center in the hypothalamus is sensitive to the amount of water in the blood, and tells you to take in fluid when the body needs it. Patterns of sleeping and waking are regulated here, as are things like heartbeat, intestinal movements and bladder-emptying.

    Your hypothalamus is the link between the nervous system (the communication system in your body that is based on nerves) and the endocrine system (which uses chemicals called hormones as its messengers). When the hypothalamus becomes aware of a physical need, it secretes chemicals that stimulate the pituitary gland.

    The posterior pituitary releases two hormones which are actually made in your hypothalamus. Oxytocin starts the process of childbirth when it is released in large quantities into the blood of a pregnant woman. It also has

**The pons**

*The pons, located just above the medulla, is the bridge between your brain and your spinal cord. It also functions as a link between different parts of your brain. Like the medulla, it consists of white nerve fibers passing up and down the brain stem, with areas of gray matter that mark the beginning of three cranial nerves.*

*    The pons' main function is to act as a major relay center linking one part of your brain to another.*

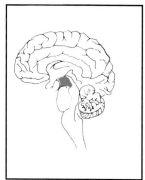

*The mid-brain*

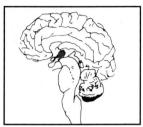

*The thalamus*

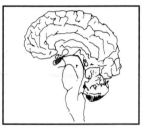

*The hypothalamus*

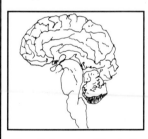

*The pituitary gland lies in the center of the brain, just behind the bridge of your nose. It is connected to the hypothalamus by a stalk-like structure. It has two portions: the anterior (front) lobe, which is made up of glandular cells, and the posterior (back) lobe, composed of nervous tissue.*

a role in milk-production. Antidiuretic hormone (ADH) prevents excessive water-loss by reducing the amount of water your kidneys remove from your blood. Without ADH, you would produce enormous quantities of urine (up to 25 liters (5.5 gallons) a day ) and lose essential salts from your blood.

Six different hormones are released by your anterior pituitary on the instruction of the hypothalamus. Most have an effect on other endocrine glands, causing them to respond by producing their own hormones (or shutting down production), but at least two, prolactin, which has to do with milk secretion, and growth hormone, which stimulates cell division, bone growth and protein synthesis, act directly on body tissues.

Your hypothalamus has been described as the link between your body and your mind. It is here that emotional changes are registered, and influence your physical state. If you see something threatening, for example, the sensation you register is fear. This emotional state is accompanied by physical changes such as an increased heartbeat, sweating, and pallor.

## Sensory organs

One of the central functions of your brain is to receive, interpret and act upon information it gains from your body's sensory organs and internal receptors. When you sense something, it is because you are being made aware of what is going on in the outside world or within your body. What your sense organs are actually reacting to, however, is change. If you get used to particular sensations - the pressure of your clothes, for example, or the temperature of your bath water - you no longer register them consciously. This is called sensory adaptation, and results from continuous stimulation at a particular level of intensity. If that level changes, it may be that your body will have to do something in order to protect itself from danger and maintain homeostasis.

Your sense organs collect information and convert it into a form which enables it to be transmitted to your brain via your nervous system. You do not feel in your

| Nerve | Type | Supplies | Function |
|-------|------|----------|----------|
| I | Sensory | Nasal receptors | Sense of smell |
| II | Sensory | Retina of eye | Vision |
| III | Motor | Four eyeball muscles, eyelids | Eyelid and eyeball movement |
| IV | Motor | One eyeball muscle | Eye movement |
| V | Sensory/Motor | Face, mouth, scalp, nose, teeth | Chewing and facial sensation |
| VI | Motor | One eyeball muscle | Eye movement |
| VII | Sensory/Motor | Face, tongue, salivary glands | Facial movement, taste |
| VIII | Sensory | Ear and organs of balance | Hearing and balance |
| IX | Sensory/Motor | Throat, tongue, salivary glands | Swallowing, taste |
| X | Sensory/Motor | Larynx, heart, stomach, intestine | Movement and internal sensation |
| XI | Motor | Head, neck, shoulder muscle | Movements |
| XII | Motor | Tongue muscles | Movements |

sense organs because they only set off the nerve impulses that tell your brain what is going on. It is up to your brain to interpret the nature of a stimulus, and where it is coming from, and then decide whether action is necessary.

Sensations can be grouped into two categories: those which are received by the general senses, and those which the special senses pick up.

## Skin sensitivity

Your skin is your largest organ. It contains many sensory receptors connected to your nervous system whose job is to keep you informed about temperature, touch and pressure.

Embedded deep in your skin are the end organs of Ruffini, receptors that are sensitive to heat changes. Ten times more numerous are the widely-distributed end bulbs of Krause, oval receptors deep within your dermis which pick up sensations of cold.

Touch receptors include networks of nerves around each of the hairs on your body, which make your skin sensitive to any kind of contact. Disc-like structures within your epidermis (the top layer of skin) called

### The cranial nerves
*There are twelve pairs of cranial nerves, ten of which originate in the brain stem, which carry messages to and from your head, neck, and most of your intestines. Each is numbered to indicate where it leaves the brain. Number I, for example, is the nerve leaving the most forward part of your brain.*

*Motor nerves go from your brain to muscles or glands, and send messages which activate them; sensory nerves take information into your brain; mixed nerves carry both sensory and motor fibers. Because your cranial nerves control conscious activities, damage to them affects your ability to use certain muscles.*

*You can check your body-position sense by holding your finger out at arm's length, closing your eyes, then bringing your finger in to touch the tip of your nose. Without looking, your brain tells your body exactly where your finger is in relationship to your nose, and you hit it spot on every time.*

Merkel's discs, also respond to touch, as do Meissner's corpuscles located just under your epidermis. Areas of your skin that are very sensitive to touch - your fingertips, for example - have many such corpuscles.

While touch sensors are generally located in the upper layers of your skin, those which register changes in pressure are deep in the dermis. These sense organs, the Pacinian corpuscles, are also present within joints, tendons and some internal organs.

## Pain sensitivity

Although sensory adaptation generally means that you get used to constant levels of stimulation until you no longer notice them, the same is not true of pain. Pain usually remains noticeable because it is a warning that something is wrong: if you ignore it, or deaden it with painkillers, you risk allowing some kind of problem to become more serious.

Pain is not always experienced in the area of the body where a problem exists. A liver complaint, for example, may cause pain across your shoulders, while pain caused by a heart problem may actually be felt across your chest and down your left arm.

Receptors that register pain are branching nerve-endings that are found in almost every tissue of your body, and they respond to almost any type of stimulus. When they are excessively stimulated, by pressure, heat or cold, for example, the result is that you feel pain.

## Body-position sensitivity

Receptors within your muscles and tendons, called proprioceptors, make you aware, by registering the tension within those structures, of what your limbs and other parts of your body are doing.

## Smell

When you breathe, you take in chemicals from the atmosphere that surrounds you. These come into contact with the mucous membrane within your nasal cavity, where they dissolve in water and bring about changes in the sensitive nerve endings there.

Information in the form of nerve impulses passes along your olfactory nerve (cranial nerve I) to your brain, which interprets it and identifies it as a particular smell.

Your sense of smell is extremely sensitive compared with your sense of taste, but it is also capable of rapid adaptation. This is why you become accustomed to a particular smell until you are no longer aware of it, while someone encountering it for the first time will notice it straight away.

Meissner's corpuscle registers touch and vibration.

## Taste

On the upper surface of your tongue, and on its sides, are papillae (bumps) you can feel when you draw your tongue through your teeth, and which contain your taste buds. Actually tasting something occurs when chemicals in your food are dissolved in saliva, stimulating the taste buds on your tongue and smell receptors in your nose. In fact, your tongue has a very limited capacity for detecting taste and different taste sensations are registered on different areas of your tongue: sweet and sour are tasted at the tip, salt and sour tastes are registered at the sides, and bitterness right at the back. It is not known why one receptor should respond to sweetness and another to bitterness. All other 'taste' sensations come through your nose.

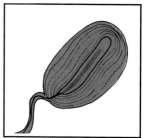

Pacinian corpuscle registers pressure.

## Vision

Your eyes are the special sense organs whose job it is to register what you see, and pass the information to your brain for interpretation. They are relatively close together at the front of your face, which means that one eye sees almost the same as the other. The two fields of vision overlap slightly: you therefore have the ability to judge distances because each eye has a view from a slightly different angle.

Your eyes are moved by six muscles attached to the outside of each eyeball. These are connected to the bony eye socket in which the eye sits, and enable the eyeball to move in different directions. If they do not move together,

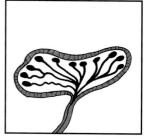

Ruffini's corpuscle registers pressure and warmth. All three receptors lie below the surface of the skin and receive information which is passed back to the brain.

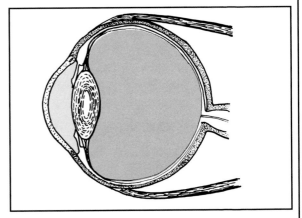

*This horizontal section of the eyeball shows the lens suspended between the aqueuous humor on the left and the vitreous humor in the main body of the eyeball. The eye receives light from objects outside. The light is 'bent' by the external tissues and internal humors of the eyeball and focused at the back of the eye on the retina.*

the result can be eyes that do not both look in the same direction.

## Protection

Your eyes are protected from damage by your eyebrows, hairy barriers above the eye that stops any sweat on your forehead rolling into your eyes. They also prevent dust falling into the eyes.

Your eyelids, folds of skin-covered muscle, can close over your eyes to protect them. Their inner surface, the conjunctiva, produces mucus to lubricate the exposed eyeball. Your eyelashes help make your eyelids sensitive to touch, so that they can close if necessary to protect your eyeball from damage caused by foreign bodies in the air nearby.

Your eyes are kept clean and lubricated by tears produced by your lacrimal (tear) glands. This fluid also contains antibacterial substances to guard against infection. Tears reach your eyeball via the lacrimal ducts leading from the glands, flow out on to the conjunctiva, and are spread when you blink. Usually the fluid drains away through the small opening you can see on the inner edge of your lower eyelid but may overflow onto your cheeks if much is produced - when you are peeling onions, for example, and your conjunctiva is irritated by the pungent juice.

## Anatomy of the eye

Your eyeball is connected directly to your brain by the thick optic nerve (cranial nerve II), and covered by three layers of tissue.

The sclera is the tough outer layer. This is the 'white' of the eye. At the front of the eyeball the sclera is transparent, and forms the cornea, which is where light passes through on its way to the inside of your eye.

The pigmented (colored) choroid layer lies beneath the sclera, and absorbs excess light which might otherwise damage your eye. It also contains the blood vessels that supply the retina.

At the front of the eyeball the choroid layer is modified to form the ciliary body, smooth muscle fibers which alter the shape of the lens when you focus on something, and the iris. Your iris (the colored part of your eye) is made of smooth muscle fieres arranged in an oval formation. It surrounds the central pupil which, though it looks like a solid black spot, is actually an opening.

Light gets into your eye via the pupil, and it is the iris that regulates the actual amount of light going through. In dim lighting, the pupil becomes bigger to allow in more light; in bright light it becomes smaller.

The retina is the innermost layer of the eyeball lining the rear portion of your eye. Its outer layer is pigmented like the choroid layer that lies next to it, while the inner part is made up of nerve cells which produce and conduct impulses to your brain via the optic nerve. Some of the nerve cells, called photoreceptors, are sensitive to light, and there are two main types: rods and cones.

Rods pick up light in dull conditions and make it possible for you to see movement and shape as well as shades of light and dark.

Cones need bright light in order to function, and act as receptors of color and sharp outline. They are mostly clustered around the central area of the retina (the yellow spot), so this is the area of sharpest vision. There are no

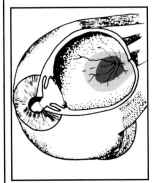

*When light enters your eye, it strikes the light-sensitive rods and cones in your retina. Rods and cones contain pigments which are broken down chemically when light strikes them. This breakdown generates the nerve impulse that carries visual information to the cerebral cortex via your optic nerve. The image you see is actually your brain's interpretation of these nerve impulses, the ordering of the information it gets when light strikes an object within your field of vision.*

rods in the yellow spot: they are found in increasing numbers towards the retina's outer edge.

Nerve impulses from both rods and cones travel along the optic nerve onwards to your brain.

On the retina, in front of the place where your optic nerve leaves your eyeball, there are neither rods nor cones. You cannot see any image focused on this part of your retina, so it is known as your blind spot.

Under the sclerotic layer at the front of your eyeball, supported by muscles of the ciliary body, is the transparent lens. Suspensory ligaments support the lens, and cause it to change shape when you focus on nearby objects or those further away.

The space within your eyeball is filled with transparent fluids, called humors, which supply nutrients and oxygen to your lens and cornea. Their pressure keeps your eyeball the right shape, and maintains the position of the retina. The watery aqueous humor circulates around your lens, while the jelly-like vitreous humor fills the chamber behind it.

## How you see

In order to see, you need light. What you recognize as a table, a friend or a bunch of flowers is actually a unique pattern of light, shade, color and movement picked up by your organ of vision (your eyes) and identified by your brain.

The various structures of your eye cooperate in order to get the light to the rods and cones. The amount of light entering your eye is determined by the size of your pupil, which is adjusted automatically by the muscles of your iris. As light passes from one medium to another (from the air into your cornea, for example), its rays are refracted (bent) slightly, and this happens again when they pass through the cornea into the aqueous humor and on through the lens into the vitreous humor.

Light rays from a distant object have to be bent only a little in order to make sure that they land on the retina, while those from near objects have to be bent more sharply - by the cornea, the humors and the lens.

If you are looking at something more than about six metres (twenty feet) away, the light from the object will enter your eye as parallel rays. These will then be refracted just enough to allow them to be focused on the most sensitive part of your retina. If you are looking at something nearer, the lens in your eye will change its shape and become fatter so that it can focus the light rays on to that sensitive spot. Although retinal images are upside-down, these cause you no problems because your brain quickly learns to interpret them so that you automatically perceive what you see the right way up.

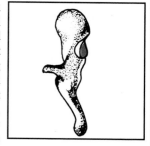
*Hammer*

# Hearing

In the same way as your eyes collect visual information that is interpreted by your brain, your ears collect auditory information: this time in the form of vibrations which are converted into nerve impulses.

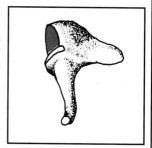

### The ear

Your ear has three main regions: the outer, middle and inner ear.

The outer ear or pinna is the bit you can see. It is *Anvil* shaped in such a way that it can pick up sounds and channel them into the external auditory canal. This canal is about 2.5 cm (1 inch) long, and leads inwards to the tympanum, your eardrum. The eardrum is a membrane which is concave on its outer surface, and which separates your outer ear from the delicate structures within.

The middle ear is a small cavity within one of your skull bones. Extending across it are three tiny bones - the malleus (hammer), the incus (anvil), and the stapes (stirrup) - which are together known as the ear ossicles. The malleus is joined to the inner surface of your eardrum, while the stapes adjoins the membrane of the oval window *Stapes* which allows vibrations to pass from the middle ear to the inner ear.

To prevent changes in external air pressure from damaging your eardrum, the middle-ear cavity is connected with your throat via the Eustachian tube. If you sense an air-pressure increase (such as might occur when

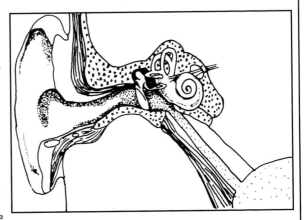

*The ear consists of an outer gristly flap and ear canal (the outer ear); a middle chamber housing the three auditory ossicles (the middle ear); and an organ of balance embedded in the bone of the skull (the inner ear). The middle ear connects with the back of the throat down the Eustachian tube. On the diagram this can be seen as an open tube running downwards. In fact, the walls of the tube lie touching each other but can be opened if the air pressure in the middle ear rises (for example, when ascending in an airplane). The air bubbles down the tube and prevents the sensitive eardrum from bulging outwards. On descent, you may have to help the tube to open to equalize the external and internal air pressure in your ear. You can do this by swallowing, yawning, biting your back teeth together, or by holding your nose and gently blowing air up your Eustachian tube.*

you are descending in a lift through a tall building), you swallow in order to let air in from your throat to the cavity of your middle ear. Yawning has the same effect.

The inner ear contains the cochlea, which is the organ of hearing, and the semi-circular canals that give you your sense of balance. The cochlea is contained in a bony spiral. Three fluid-filled channels (the scala vestibuli, the scala tympani and the cochlear duct) are separated by the vestibular membrane. Inside the cochlea is the sound receptor, the organ of Corti, which consists of nerve cells (called hair cells) resting on the basilar membrane. Over the top of the hair cells is another membrane, the tectorial, that touches their tips when vibrations run through the cochlear duct.

### Hearing
When a stone drops into a pond, waves travel across the water. Sound travels through the air in much the same way. Sound waves, felt as vibrations, arrive at he eardrum. It vibrates in sympathy, then its movements are transmitted to the cochlea by means of the ear ossicles and the oval window. In effect, this means that air movements turn into bone movements which, in turn, become movements of the fluid inside the cochlea.

## Balance

Your ears contain your organs of hearing, but they also contain structures responsible for helping you keep your balance both when still and on the move.

Your static sense of balance keeps your body steady and upright when you are not moving. It depends on the proper functioning of two structures closely connected to the semi-circular canals of your inner ear, two sacs filled with endolymph called the sacculus and utriculus. Projecting into them are hair cells surrounded by a jelly-like substance, and in this substance are embedded tiny otoliths (stones) made from calcium carbonate.

When you move your head from an upright position, the stones move and nudge the hairs on the nerve cells. As the hairs bend, they cause a nervous impulse to travel to the brain which then organizes any necessary corrective actions.

Your dynamic sense of balance - the kind of facility you need if you stumble or trip, for example - is the function of the semi-circular canals themselves. These are set at right-angles to each other. At the base of each is a swelling which contains a crista (sense organ; plural cristae) made up of hair cells which stick out into the endolymph that fills the canal.

If your head moves fast in one direction, the endolymph in your semi-circular canals also moves. It sweeps over the nerve cells of the cristae and, as their hair cells bend, nerve impulses are sent to the brain.

## Communications between body and brain

All your sense organs are connected either to your brain or to your spinal cord (your central nervous system) by nerve fibers. When a sense organ receives a stimulus it sets off a burst of electrical impulses in the nerve fiber supplying it. Impulses travel along the nerve fiber, sometimes producing an automatic or reflex action, at others recording an impression which means that you consciously experience the nature and source of the stimulus as sensation.

Far more stimuli reach your brain than you could

*A noise produces the following sequence of events inside your head:*

*1. Sound waves (vibrations in the air) reach your head, are collected up by the outer ear and channeled into your external auditory canal.*

*2. The vibrations hit the eardrum and make it vibrate.*

*3. As the eardrum vibrates, it moves the malleus bone, thus passing the vibrations on to the other ear ossicles (the incus and stapes).*

*4. As the stapes moves, it pushes against the membrane covering the oval window. As the membrane moves, waves of vibration are transmitted to the fluid inside the inner ear.*

*5. When the perilymph (the fluid inside the scala vestibuli) moves, it presses against the vestibular membrane and so comes into contact with the endolymph fluid within the cochlear duct.*

*6. The movement of endolymph makes the basilar membrane vibrate. As it does so, it causes the organ of Corti's nerve hairs to hit the tectorial membrane, and nerve impulses are generated in the auditory nerve (cranial nerve VIII).*

ever hope, or need, to be aware of. You do not need to make conscious adjustments to compensate for changes in the pressure or carbon dioxide content of your blood, for example. This kind of information never reaches conscious levels, and any necessary action is taken automatically.

## Your nervous system

What is called for convenience your nervous system is actually a number of interlinked ones.

• Your **central nervous system** consists of your brain and spinal cord.

• Your **peripheral nervous system** consists of the nerve pathways that run between your central nervous system and the organs and muscles of your body.

• Your **autonomic nervous system** is that part of your peripheral nervous system which is responsible for monitoring and controlling all the activities of your internal organs, and which does this without your conscious control. This system is further broken down into the parasympathetic division responsible for normal rest and repair activities, and the sympathetic division which takes over when emergency action - 'fight or flight', for example - is required. Both function automatically and unconsciously.

## Your endocrine system

One of the characteristics of your nervous system is its ability to respond rapidly to all sorts of stimuli. Your endocrine system, on the other hand, has to do with those of your body's activities which are continuous over a long period of time.

Endocrine glands produce hormones, chemical messengers that are transported around your body in your blood. When they reach their destination, they cause particular changes to take place. Their effects are slower and more general than those brought about by nerve action: among the long-term changes they control are growth, sexual maturity and your reproductive system.

An elaborate feedback mechanism ensures that hormone production is carefully regulated. Its effectiveness comes from the close relationship between the pituitary gland (sometimes called the 'master gland' because of its central role in influencing the activities of the rest of the endocrine system) and the hypothalamus (see page 13) which monitors the levels of the various hormones in circulation throughout your body.

Although the pituitary stimulates the other endocrine glands into action by means of hormones, it is itself stimulated by nerve impulses from the hypothalamus.

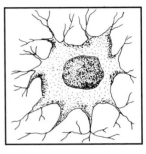

*The basic unit on which your nervous system is built is the neurone, or nerve cell. These vary in size and shape depending on where they are and what they have to do, but all have a nucleus surrounded by a cell body.*

## Neurones and nerves

Coming out from the cell body are branching nerve fibers which either bring messages in to the cell body, pass them to other neurones, or transmit them away from the cell body. Neurones are therefore of three main types:

Sensory neurones carry information into your brain and spinal cord from your sense organs or receptors.

Association neurones found in your brain and spinal cord form links between sensory and motor neurones.

Motor neurones carry messages away from your brain and spinal cord to your muscles and glands. They motivate organs into action. The muscles in your arms, for example, move because of messages reaching them by way of motor neurones.

Humans' nerve cell bodies are mostly found in the brain and spinal cord, though their fibers extend all the way to the organ from which they are receiving information, or which they are activating. Fibers may therefore be very long, stretching all the way from the spinal cord to the toe or fingertip, for example. Hundreds of fibers are bound together to form nerves.

### Transmitting information

Although nerve fibers communicate with the brain, with one another, and with muscles and glands, they do not

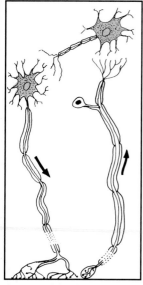

*Axons and dendrites*

actually touch. The tiny gap between one neurone's axon (the fiber which transmits information away from a cell body) and another's dendron (the fiber that brings information into a cell body) is called a synapse. The similar gap between a motor neurone's axon and the muscle or gland it activates is the myoneural junction. Information is passed from one cell to another, or from a motor neurone to the muscle it affects, when an electrical charge builds up within the fiber and a particular threshold of stimulation is reached. At that time, an electrical impulse is released. This travels along the neurone's axon until it reaches its branched endings - and the synapse or myoneural junction.

When the impulse arrives at the bump-like synaptic knobs on the end of the axon, a chemical called a neurotransmitter is released. This travels across the synapse or myoneural junction to stimulate either the next neurone or the muscle it has reached. Messages flash along nerve fibers at speeds of up to 130 meters per second.

Whether information is traveling from sensory organs to your brain, from one cell to another within your brain, or out from your central nervous system with an instruction for action, the process is the same.

# Healthy mind

• *Counseling and self-help*
*There are various ways to deal with mental health problems which have arisen from no particular theory, but which just seem to be a 'common-sense' answer to a particular problem. Many sorts of counseling and self-help groups seem to fall into this category. On closer inspection the insight which led to the development of these techniques usually turns out to be far from common, and the sense which led to their creation was often derived from one or other of the theoretical systems outlined in this section. However, they are sometimes hard to categorize.*

• *Religion*
*In many parts of the world this too has traditionally had something to say about what mental health is and how to achieve it. In our cosmopolitan world many different aspects of these religious approaches are available, with or without the religion from which they originally sprung. Meditation, Christian or Buddhist; Tai Chi and Yoga are examples of religious or semi-religious techniques which are held to have mental-health-promoting effects.*

It is very straightforward to advise on how to keep your body healthy. It is much harder to define how the brain works, and to decide what we mean by mental health. The part of medicine known as psychiatry is concerned with this subject. Psychology is a different discipline which has developed separately from psychiatry, although they overlap and borrow ideas from each other. The 'academic parents' of psychology are philosophy and physiology.

Since the Ancient Greeks, philosophy has been concerned with questions like what is the purpose of life, what are emotions, and memory, how can one find happiness, how do we know things, and what is the relationship between the mental and the physical worlds?

Physiology developed more recently, in an attempt to discover how the body works. The attempt to extend the methods used in the study of the brain to the study of the mind led to the development of scientific psychology at the end of the nineteenth century. Matters previously thought of as part of philosophy began to be studied scientifically.

Because the mind is such a complex subject of study, there are many different 'schools' of psychology, or the use of different 'models', as these different approaches are sometimes called.

## Psychiatry

Psychiatry developed as an off-shoot of neurology, that part of medicine which deals with disorders of the nervous system. Like other branches of medicine, it uses physical methods of treatment (principally drugs) although many other approaches have been adopted by psychiatrists from psychology and other disciplines. Like practitioners of other branches of medicine, psychiatrists tend to think in terms of diagnosis, illness, prognosis and treatment.

Psychiatrists divide mental illnesses into neurotic and psychotic. People with neurotic illness have 'insight' into their condition. To some extent they can agree with other people about the nature of their situation, and retain a degree of rationality. Anxiety and depression are the commonest neurotic conditions. Neurotic illnesses can

*Karl Rogers developed client-centered therapy aimed at self-actualization, i.e. achieving the full growth of which people are capable. It is non-directive counseling. The therapist provides a warm and empathic milieu in which people can explore their inner feelings, but makes no attempt to direct the client. Instead the latter is encouraged to continue talking as the therapist makes sympathetic noises, or rephrases what has been said in another way, or as a question. Thus the person undergoing therapy sets the entire agenda for the interaction, and the therapist merely enables them to develop in the ways that are right for them.*

*Freud believed that the mind could be seen as involving three elements:*
*• The **ego** is the self of which we are often conscious.*
*• The **id** contains our inner, primitive drives for biological and personal gratification, which motivate our actions, and which are controlled and rendered acceptable by the ego.*
*• The **superego** is an internalization of our parents' influence which controls us, not by the light of reason as does the ego, but by guilt and repression.*

be seen as excesses of normal human emotions, thus anxiety as an illness is merely an extreme version of normal nervousness and worries. In fact, the boundary between the two is rather vague.

Psychotic illnesses are characterized by a lack of insight, a breakdown in rationality and a failure to agree about the nature of the problem with those around. False and unshakable beliefs, and bizarre interpretations of events, hallucinations and delusions are often seen in such conditions. This is generally what the layperson means by madness, although this vague term is not used in psychiatry or psychology. Schizophrenia and manic and depressive psychoses are the most important illnesses of this nature.

## Psychoanalysis

The founder of psychoanalysis was Sigmund Freud, a Viennese neurologist at the end of the nineteenth century. His theory was developed to explain the neurotic illnesses which were presented to him in his practice as a neurologist, and which he could not explain in terms of the ideas current at the time.

Freud proposed that the foundations of personality were laid down in early childhood. He suggested that the development of an understanding of these inner processes, with the help of the therapist in analysis, using techniques such as dream recall and free association, would enable individuals to resolve their inner conflicts and thus cure their neuroses.

Freud was, and remains, a controversial figure. That he has permanently altered the way we look at things is however unquestionable. The notions of the unconscious mind; the importance of emotional childhood experiences in shaping later behavior; and the role of self-understanding in promoting mental health are accepted by many who would not in any way consider themselves to be Freudians.

Amongst the many people who have developed, changed and refined Freud's ideas the most prominent is Carl Gustav Jung, a Swiss psychiatrist. He was much less scientific and more mystical, even religious in his understanding of the psyche.

As well as developments in the theory there have been developments in the practice of psychoanalyis. Classical Freudian analysis is individual and prolonged, making it expensive and impractical for most people, and shorter methods using groups have been developed. Anyone considering psychoanalyis thus has a bewildering range of theoretical approaches and methods to choose from, and will need to make careful enquiry to discover what will suit them best.

## Cognitive-behavioral psychology

Whilst Freud and his followers were attempting to fathom the unconscious minds of their patients, scientific psychologists were concerned with theoretical issues to do with learning. They discovered that animals and humans share common principles which govern how they learn. They then applied this knowledge to the problems dealt with by psychiatry, which they saw as due to wrong patterns of learning, and referred to as behavior disorders rather than mental illnesses.

> • **Psychology** is the study of the normal mind.
>
> • **Psychiatry** is the study of the diseased mind.

There are several classes of drugs which can be helpful to people suffering from mental illness.

• **Tranquilizers**
These are sometimes referred to as minor tranquilizers and exert a generally calming effect, decreasing anxiety. Similar drugs administered in large doses with a short action are known as sedatives, used to promote sleep (see pages 44-46).

• **Antidepressants**
Quite different in their effect are the antidepressant drugs. They are not addictive, although some of them have a sedative effect, and are given in a daily dose at night for this reason (see pages 52-53).

• **Antipsychotic drugs**
The third group of drugs are the major tranquilizers, or antipsychotic drugs (see pages 61-63).

• **Electroconvulsive therapy**
Another treatment which is powerful but widely distrusted is electroconvulsive therapy or ECT (see page 64).

## Methods used in cognitive-behavioral psychology

*These are very different from those of the analysts. The principle that anxiety, depression, obsessions etc are due to incorrect learning, and that what can be learnt can be unlearnt, remains the cornerstone of the theory. The emphasis is on observable and measurable behavior, rather than on the hidden mysteries of the unconscious, although mental activity and thought (long considered to be unmeasurable) are now studied and measured in the same way as more obvious behavior; hence the term cognitive-behavioral. The psychologist is much more likely to accept the problem as the patient defines it at its face value, and tackle what she or he sees in the present, rather than concentrating on the roots of the problem in the distant past. Although the psychologist will try to help patients to understand why they behave as they do, this insight is not the aim of therapy, but a means to an end. Once the problem has been analyzed, the therapist will teach the patient skills to use to overcome the unwanted behavior patterns - to control panic attacks, for example, or to deal with depressing thoughts.*

Unlike psychoanalysts, who see their work as too subtle and individual to be evaluated other than by description of the individual case, cognitive-behavioral psychologists have been keen to test their techniques scientifically. For this reason there is more concrete evidence for the success of these treatments than in almost any other area of mental health. Treatments have been developed - and shown good results - for anxiety, depression, phobias, obsessions and for sexual problems. Of course, whether one accepts the psychologist's pragmatic definition of success is a matter of personal choice.

# Humanistic theories

A group of theorists who would probably not do so are the humanistic psychologists. This term covers a disparate collection of psychotherapists who are concerned with promoting the personal development of their clients, in a rather wider sense than the mental-illness treatment of psychiatry, or the modification of behavior disorders of the clinical psychologist. They share with psychoanalysis an origin in the attempt to help people with emotional problems, but adopt different models of the human mind.

Rational emotive therapy is somewhat at the opposite end of the spectrum. The principle behind this form of treatment is that many emotional crises are irrational and illogical. By pointing out to oneself the true logic of the situation, one can overcome emotional problems by literally talking oneself out of them. The therapist encourages and supports as well as teaches the client how to do this.

Kelly invented personal construct theory in the 1950s. He formed the view that the best way to see man is as a scientist, trying to make sense of his world. Just as scientists develop theories, so people develop constructs, which they use to categorize things and to make sense of the world. Constructs usually consist of two opposite poles; thus good/bad, happy/sad, successful/unsuccessful are examples of constructs used to evaluate actions or people, the 'element' over which the construct has a 'range of convenience', thus one can describe a person, or a day, as happy, but it makes little sense to talk of a happy lettuce. Lettuce is an element outside the range of convenience of the construct happy/sad.

Kelly developed ways of measuring the relationship between the constructs which an individual uses, and described the ways in which they change, and the effects of their changes for an individual. Since for the Kellian the world only exists as defined by a person's construct system, the aim of psychotherapy is to help someone to develop their construct system in such a way as to remove whatever problems they currently have in using it.

These humanistic psychologists, although they have not produced large bodies of people and research, as have cognitive-behavioral psychology and psychoanalysis, have contributed much to psychotherapy in general.

*Yoga is another form of meditative exercise which has become popular largely as a system of exercises to develop relaxation and suppleness of the body, but in its native India it is seen as a spiritual as well as a physical exercise.*

## Types of therapy

So far we have discussed the different theories which people who offer psychological treatment or therapy might hold. Equally important are the different ways in which they may work, which is quite independent of their philosophical approach.

The most traditional way of working is with one therapist and one patient or client, and this is still the most common. However, this is very expensive and time-consuming, so various forms of group therapy have been developed. These may be analytic groups or behavioral groups, organized around topics such as assertiveness, or social skills. It has been realized that this is not only an economical way for one therapist to help a number of clients but the group itself may be of therapeutic benefit. The most extreme development of this aspect of group work is the self-help group.

These have developed largely in the last thirty years, although some organizations which work in the same way are much older. The essence of a self-help group is that people have the innate ability to help each other to solve problems; a professional therapist is not essential. *(Continued on page 34.)*

# Relaxation

*Relaxation techniques all teach you to be aware of the tension in your body so that you can concentrate on relaxing the muscles. Ideally, you should practise relaxation in a quiet room, preferably somewhere you can lie down. However, this is often not convenient. Once you have learnt good relaxation techniques, you can use them for 'spot relaxation' if you feel tension building up. These four exercises can help relieve tension headaches. Hunch your shoulders up towards your ears (1), then drop them down (2). Imagine that your shoulders feel heavy. Repeat five times. Gently tip your head forward (3) and feel the muscles pulling up through the middle of your shoulder blades. Move your head gently backwards (4) and feel the tension in the muscles down the front of the neck. Do this gently four more times before bringing your head to an upright position, taking a deep breath, and breathing out deeply.*

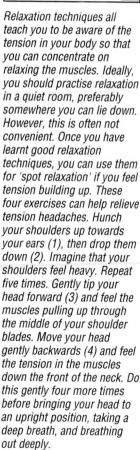

## Relaxation

What many of these activities share is a calming of the activity of the body and of the nervous system achieved often by controlling breathing and/or relaxing movements of the body. This sort of relaxation training can be done quite apart from any religious system, and is often taught by physiotherapists, psychologists and doctors. (Of course even the religious types of meditation do not necessarily demand that one accepts the whole theory of the religion in order to benefit from their practices; one merely has to be prepared to accept that the practice itself can be beneficial.)

A common practice in many religions which has much to commend it for mental health is the retreat. In a retreat people go away to a quiet place, leaving their daily life, and devote their time to prayer and quiet activities. Often they will give up talking entirely for a few days to exploit the opportunity for silence. Such periods of tranquility can be very helpful in relieving tension and anxiety.

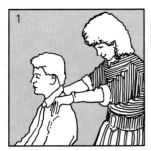
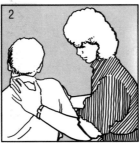

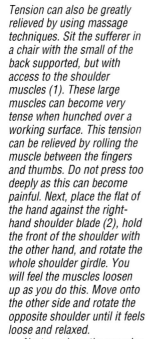

Tension can also be greatly relieved by using massage techniques. Sit the sufferer in a chair with the small of the back supported, but with access to the shoulder muscles (1). These large muscles can become very tense when hunched over a working surface. This tension can be relieved by rolling the muscle between the fingers and thumbs. Do not press too deeply as this can become painful. Next, place the flat of the hand against the right-hand shoulder blade (2), hold the front of the shoulder with the other hand, and rotate the whole shoulder girdle. You will feel the muscles loosen up as you do this. Move onto the other side and rotate the opposite shoulder until it feels loose and relaxed.

Next, work on the muscles of the back which run beside the shoulder blades (3). Hold the top of the muscle in your left hand, and work the thumb of the other hand gently along the edge of the shoulder blade, downward towards the heart. Use circular movements and apply increasing amounts of pressure as you feel the muscle relax underneath your hand.

Finally, work on the muscles at the back of the neck where they join the skull (4). A number of migraine sufferers find that this type of neck massage, accompanied by scalp massage, greatly relieves headaches. Place your thumb on one side of the neck, your fingers on the other, and support the relaxed head on your other hand. Work your fingers and thumb together in a circular movement, gently moving up towards the scalp until you reach the base of the skull. Begin again at the base of the neck, and work upwards. Having completed five upward sweeps, move the circular massaging motion up onto the scalp, feeling the skin of the scalp moving over the skull beneath. You may find it easier to use both hands to do this. The action is similar to that used when massaging shampoo into the scalp. Work from back to front, then around and down to the temples. Be guided by what is comfortable for the sufferer. Some people find that hard pressure is very relieving, while other people prefer a gentle, more rhythmic motion.

**Choosing a holiday**
*The wise person chooses the holiday which complements the usual run of daily life. The person whose job is physically strenuous may benefit from lying on a beach, whilst someone with a repetitive job may prefer an adventure or activity holiday. A mentally taxing job may indicate a physically strenuous holiday and so on.*

*The same applies to weekends, short breaks and even evenings or other periods of leisure. A contrasting hobby which stimulates the mind or body in a different way from work is often mentally beneficial. As the old but true saying goes 'A change is as good as a rest'.*

This is particularly true of those who have shared similar experiences, and so self-help groups are organized around particular issues; parents who have lost children through cot deaths, people who have suffered from agoraphobia, problems with alcohol, being a single parent, or caring for a sick relative etc. They usually meet as a group, often quite informally to talk, perhaps with help from appropriate specialists but more often to share experiences and support each other. These have proved extremely valuable, and there are now self-help groups for almost any illness or stressful experience in life one could think of.

## Religious approaches

So far we have looked at the ways science, through medicine or through the academic study of the mind, has attempted to help people deal with mental anguish, unwanted behavior or antisocial tendencies. It is a truism that such healing attempts antedate modern science by several thousand years.

Many of the world's religions have developed techniques which are designed to help you to have a calm, peaceful attitude to life, and to help deal with its crises. In the last twenty years various Oriental forms of meditation have become popular in the West such as transcendental meditation and Tai Chi, a Chinese form of meditation involving slow and deliberate movements, which is linked to the more vigorous martial arts from the same culture. Buddhism too has systems of meditation which can be learnt.

These recent imports have tended to overshadow the meditative tradition of the Christian religion, which also has methods of dealing with tension and mental stress. There is a variety of types of prayer which are designed to produce a state of deep peace and calm in the person praying. Of course this was not always the main purpose of these things, and not all religion is about calm and peace, but many people, even if not holding any particular religious belief themselves, can find these things helpful in promoting their own inner calm and relaxation.

Amongst recreational activities with health benefits, of particular importance is exercise. Vigorous physical exertion is followed by a converse deep physical relaxation which can dissipate tension.

Most people in modern societies do not have jobs which are physically strenuous enough to provide the exercise needed for physical and mental health. Being busy is not a substitute for some activity which raises the pulse and respiration rate. Some forms of exercise seem to be more beneficial than others. Swimming seems to be particularly useful, but running, walking and cycling are also found to be of use by some people. Competitive exercise, although it may be very enjoyable, is not usually particularly relaxing, and indeed may add to nervous tension if the stakes are high.

# Rest and recreation

A secular activity which can be the equivalent to the religious retreat is the holiday. Not all holidays are good for mental health (they can be stresses in themselves) but for many people a holiday, or even just a day off, can relieve stress to a remarkable degree. Overwork, and lack of a proper balance between different activities physical and mental, work and leisure, is a common cause of physical and mental illness (see left-hand column).

You will see that if you wish to look after your mental health, or deal with problems which you feel you have in your life in this area, there are a wide variety of options open. There is no single magic answer for everyone, but rather a variety of things which may help different people at different times. In the next two sections we will look at some of the problems people have with their mental health, and deliberate which of the therapies or activities we have been discussing might help them.

If you wish to pursue any of the topics mentioned in this chapter further, there is a list of addresses at the end of the book.

# Migraine

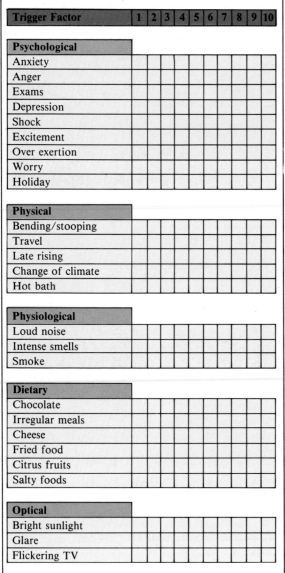

| Trigger Factor | 1 | 2 | 3 | 4 | 5 | 6 | 7 | 8 | 9 | 10 |
|---|---|---|---|---|---|---|---|---|---|---|
| **Psychological** | | | | | | | | | | |
| Anxiety | | | | | | | | | | |
| Anger | | | | | | | | | | |
| Exams | | | | | | | | | | |
| Depression | | | | | | | | | | |
| Shock | | | | | | | | | | |
| Excitement | | | | | | | | | | |
| Over exertion | | | | | | | | | | |
| Worry | | | | | | | | | | |
| Holiday | | | | | | | | | | |
| **Physical** | | | | | | | | | | |
| Bending/stooping | | | | | | | | | | |
| Travel | | | | | | | | | | |
| Late rising | | | | | | | | | | |
| Change of climate | | | | | | | | | | |
| Hot bath | | | | | | | | | | |
| **Physiological** | | | | | | | | | | |
| Loud noise | | | | | | | | | | |
| Intense smells | | | | | | | | | | |
| Smoke | | | | | | | | | | |
| **Dietary** | | | | | | | | | | |
| Chocolate | | | | | | | | | | |
| Irregular meals | | | | | | | | | | |
| Cheese | | | | | | | | | | |
| Fried food | | | | | | | | | | |
| Citrus fruits | | | | | | | | | | |
| Salty foods | | | | | | | | | | |
| **Optical** | | | | | | | | | | |
| Bright sunlight | | | | | | | | | | |
| Glare | | | | | | | | | | |
| Flickering TV | | | | | | | | | | |

*Classic migraine headaches affect one side of the head and are associated with nausea and vomiting as well as temporary changes in vision. These vision changes may occur before the attack (and herald it), may occur during the attack, and may linger as an 'aura' for twenty-four hours after an attack. They include scintilla (flashing bright lights), tunnel vision and haloes of light around objects.*

*An attack of migraine is triggered by different things for different people. Isolating that trigger helps one to avoid attacks, but often a single trigger is not enough. If you fill in the chart on the left-hand side for ten different migraine attacks, a pattern will emerge and you may well find that although you have always regarded chocolate as being the single trigger, it only triggers an attack if you eat it when you're feeling* depressed, or under more stress than usual.

Once an attack is under way, you must find remedies to lessen the symptoms. Acupressure may help - roll the band of muscle between your thumb and fingers (top left). The pressure should be hard enough to cause pain.

One of the problems with taking medication for migraine is that once vomiting sets in you cannot absorb the medication. Suppositories are one answer, but many people find these unacceptable. Medication to prevent vomiting is now available for absorption through the mucous membrane of the mouth. The pill is placed between gum and lip and absorbed directly into the blood stream. Once the vomiting has been stemmed, ordinary painkillers can be taken by mouth to combat the pain of the migraine.

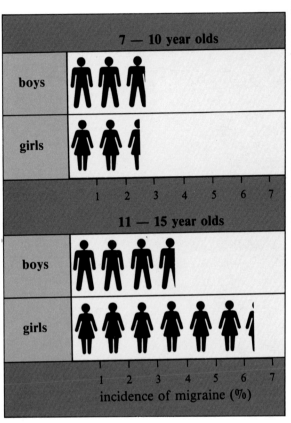

incidence of migraine (%)

Headaches are very common in childhood and the word migraine is often used loosely. Many headaches described as migraines are in fact tension headaches. Children do suffer migraine attacks, but the symptoms are often not the same as adults. They may manifest themselves as 'abdominal migraine', recurrent bouts of painful but unexplained tummy ache, sometimes with vomiting.

The chart above shows that up to the age of ten, boys and girls tend to suffer equally from migraine, but the moment children reach puberty, the incidence of migraine rapidly rises among the girls. It also rises in boys, but not to such an extend.

# Influencable conditions

Most people suffer minor psychological distress from time to time. This may be because becoming anxious or depressed is part' of their personality, or because of traumatic events in their lives. Dealing with this sort of minor illness involves understanding the way you tend to react to stress, and what are the likely causes of such stress, as well as knowing what ways of dealing with them area available.

In this section the common causes of minor psychological illness, distress or nervous illness (a variety of terms is used interchangeably) will be discussed. The two major types of nervous reaction, anxiety and depression, will then be described, together with the various sorts of treatment available. Finally we will consider other steps which can be taken to avoid nervous illness.

## Causes of minor mental illness

Although some people are constitutionally more vulnerable to stress than others, and what affects one individual may affect another much less, according to their personality, there are a few common situations which are likely to be stressful.

Personal relationships are perhaps the most important single cause of stress. The loss of a significant relationship, whether through death or through separation, is always painful, and provokes a bereavement reaction. The normal bereavement reaction includes three stages - denial, anger and acceptance. First the person is unable to accept the loss, it doesn't seem real. Then it becomes only too real, and anger is felt. Why should this happen to me? Why did God, or the people involved, behave so stupidly? This anger may be turned inwards, causing guilt and depression. Did I do all I could to prevent this terrible thing happening? I must be an awful person to deserve this suffering. Finally the sufferer adjusts to the loss, and although sadness often remains, life can again be lived and enjoyed. These feelings, usually described as stages occurring one after another, are in reality often mixed up, and one moves backwards and forwards between them.

Although the loss of a relationship is the commonest cause of the bereavement reaction in its fullest sense, many people experience similar feelings on losing a job or an opportunity, or any similar disappointment. Changes of any sort often produce bereavement, often mixed up with uncertainty as to what the future holds. Adolescence, early stages in a career or a marriage, the point when children grow up and no longer require a lot of caring for, retirement and the point (often when an illness is diagnosed) when people find they have to face up to their eventual death, are all major points in life where loss and uncertainty occur and cause stress. Moving house, a seemingly unemotional and practical activity, is in fact one of the major changes in life likely to produce emotional illness.

People often think of psychological stress as being related to childhood experience, because of the influence of psychoanalysis, and it is true that for some people a major crisis in their lives, or a series of more minor ones, is largely caused by their attempt to come to terms with their relationship with their parents. Jung said we spend the first half of our lives becoming independent of our parents and the second half preparing for death - a true if slightly pessimistic summary of the human condition.

The other major cause of emotional illness is overload. This can be too much work, too much responsibility, or even just too much activity in general, even if much of it is pleasurable. It may also be the summation of very many minor irritations and annoyances, none of them in themselves of any major importance, but which together add up to a major stress. This may build up gradually with no stress consciously felt until after months or even years of dealing with an excessive burden.

Although there is a wide variety of causes of nervous illness, there is a remarkable similarity in the symptoms which such illnesses cause. There is no clear dividing line between minor mental illness (or neurotic illnesses as psychiatrists call them) and normal mental life. It is human nature to be worried when faced with uncertainty, depressed when a relationship or a job is lost, and so on. It is merely the frequency and severity of these feelings which distinguish those who seek medical treatment or therapy from those who just see them as part of everyday life.

Conversely, this means that the treatments or preventative measures which have been designed for those with severe problems can be used or adapted for helping all of us to cope with the problems of everyday life better. Whilst it is true that worry and depression are part of life, it is equally certain that there are some ways of dealing with these things, and the stresses which cause them, which are better than others. Many people complicate their lives still further by dealing with psychological stress in the wrong way - for example drinking alcohol to deal with depression, which makes it worse. Also much distress is caused by people not understanding their feelings, and being concerned that they are abnormal, and perhaps that they are going mad.

## Anxiety

Of all forms of psychological distress, anxiety is the most universal. There can be few if any people, no matter how laid back, who have not at some time or other worried about an examination result, shortage of money, or what someone they value thinks of them.

Mild degrees of anxiety indeed are useful. Our performance is rather better if we are a little keyed up - our concentration is improved, and our physical performance is just that bit better than usual. If, however, the anxiety becomes too great then performance deteriorates and we are unable to concentrate.

There are also degrees of appropriateness of anxiety. Although a useful emotional state, anxiety is not pleasant. If it is experienced at rare important events such as competitions or interviews it is acceptable; if however every trip to the shops is fraught with anxiety (Will I forget something? Will I get run over? Will I be late) life becomes intolerable. If the frequency or the severity of anxiety is such as to prevent the enjoyment of all or part of life, there are steps which can be taken to reduce it.

## What causes anxiety?

Anxiety is a complex phenomenon, with both physical and mental aspects. The physical changes of acute anxiety are often described as the fight or flight reaction. When faced with a sudden threat, the body reacts by a set of changes designed to prepare for immediate violent physical activity, as required for a fight or for running away. The breathing and heart rates increase, to provide more oxygen to fuel the body's activities; the blood supply to the muscles increases and they tense up, ready for rapid movement. Activity of the bowels also increases, and the pupils dilate and sweating occurs. These changes are all produced by an increase in the activity of the sympathetic nervous system, part of the body's control mechanism which works subconsciously under normal circumstances.

Associated with the physical reactions of acute anxiety are mental changes. Psychologists use the concept of 'arousal' to describe the mental changes of anxiety. The more aroused a person is, the quicker everything happens, and the higher the general background level of activity. Arousal is linked to performance by an inverted U-shaped curve. Clearly if we are very sluggish and even sleepy, then we will perform poorly and reactions will be slow. Up to a certain point, which varies between individuals but usually involves a certain level of anxiety, performance and speed of reactions increase. This explains the need to be keyed up to do well described above. If the level of arousal goes too high, however, behavior becomes confused and disorganized, and performance drops. One can easily think of examples of such a situation: the child paralysed by fright, unable to speak, or the person who is so tense that he or she is unable to concentrate, flitting from activity to activity or topic to topic without achieving anything.

Different people have different optimum levels of arousal for efficient and comfortable working. It is common knowledge that some people perform better under pressure, whilst others do better in a calmer situation. For some people at some times, their degree of arousal is excessive and is experienced as one of the various forms of anxiety.

## Types of anxiety

Specific anxiety is a common pattern. People often experience this when faced with some uncertainty or upset about something important in their lives. They find themselves worrying about it and becoming over-aroused. They are unable to prevent thoughts about the problem running through their minds. Sleep is often disturbed, and the physical symptoms of anxiety described above may be experienced. Rationally the sufferer is often aware that, whatever the outcome of the problem, it is unlikely to be influenced by worrying. This rational knowledge does not prevent worry.

For many people such anxiety is a temporary consequence of major upsets in life which occur rarely. For more anxiety-prone individuals it can be a regular feature of their lives, precipitated by trivial events. The extreme example of this situation is called 'free-floating anxiety' where the person is in a continuous state of anxiety and over-arousal, but is unable to identify any clear reason for unease.

Insomnia is a common feature of all types of anxiety, and may be the thing which most bothers the patient. The anxious thoughts run through the head, preventing the onset of sleep, and the physical over-arousal leads the body to toss and turn rather than quieten down as is usual prior to sleep. The reticular activating system, the part of the brain which usually keeps us awake during the day and shuts down at night to allow sleep to occur, remains active.

## Somatic anxiety

The majority of sufferers from anxiety will identify it as such. Some, however, experience the physical changes of increased arousal, but fail to recognize the cause. Instead they notice a dysfunction in their bodies and become concerned that they may have an illness. They may focus on the increased rate and force of the heartbeat and wonder if they have heart disease, or the increase in rate of breathing and think there is something wrong with their lungs.

The blood supply to the stomach and bowels, and the secretion of gastric acid, is affected by emotion, and these psychosomatic aspects of anxiety can often lead to symptoms in this area. Nervous indigestion causes a vague pain in the top part of the stomach, whereas the irritable bowel syndrome often caused by stress is due to overactivity of the lower part of the bowel. The bowel contents are hurried through this part of the digestive system, preventing the proper absorption of water and leading to excessively frequent loose bowel movements.

All these symptoms, although they are commonly caused by anxiety, can have other causes. Sufferers are usually well aware of this, and since an anxiety state predisposes one to fear the worst, they usually assume that the more pessimistic diagnosis is the correct one. Their anxiety about serious physical illness is added to the original stress, making the whole situation worse and forming a vicious circle.

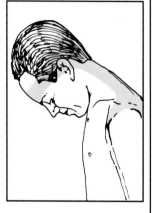

*The changes in muscle tension can produce a variety of symptoms which resemble physical illnesses. The tension headache is probably the commonest of these. This is experienced as a tight band around the head, usually equally severe on both sides, either mainly at the front of the head, or stretching back to the muscles in the back of the neck. Other common sites of nervous muscular tension are the shoulder and neck muscles, and the low back. Sometimes the tension is general throughout the body, and in association with disturbed or broken sleep produces symptoms of aching and tiredness*

## Acute anxiety

All the above types of anxiety symptom are chronic, in the sense that they last at least for a few hours. Another aspect of the same condition is acute anxiety. These reactions may only last a few minutes, but although very short are correspondingly severe.

The most extreme example of this type of reaction is the panic attack. Often occurring in people who also have more chronic symptoms of anxiety, it may happen out of the blue in someone who does not feel anxious at other times. The panic attack closely resembles the acute flight or fight reaction described above. Breathing and pulse rate increase, the person becomes sweaty, and the stomach churns over.

A particular type of panic attack is the acute hyperventilation episode. In this the breathing pattern becomes so abnormal, with rapid, shallow gasping breaths, that the biochemical balance of the blood is upset. The

A fear of snakes has some rational basis, but often phobias have no element of useful self-preservation - for example, fear of spiders.

carbon dioxide, which normally makes the blood slightly acid, is removed more quickly than usual and the blood becomes excessively alkaline. This upsets the distribution of calcium in the nerves and muscles, and bizarre symptoms occur in these tissues. In mild attacks this takes the form of pins and needles in the hands and lips; in more severe episodes the muscles of the hands and face may actually go into spasms which are very painful. Once this process starts the experience of loss of control of the body is very frightening, and this adds to the anxiety, making the symptoms worse.

## Phobias

A particular form of acute anxiety which deserves special mention is the phobic reaction. Most people have specific fears, which are more or less rational. Fear of heights, fear of enclosed spaces and fear of snakes are common phobias which have an element of useful self-preservation about them. For some people such strong fears become attached to objects and situations which either carry no real risk -fear of butterflies or spiders, for example - or become irrational in their intensity. Examples of the latter situation are someone who, for fear of driving too fast, is prevented from using motorways at all, or someone whose rational caution of vicious dogs extends to a harmless chihuahua.

In all these cases exposure to the feared stimulus produces symptoms of acute anxiety, which may vary in intensity from a vague unease to a full-blown panic attack. In consequence it is usual for the sufferer to avoid the feared situation. In many cases this is possible with little or no inconvenience; in others it can be seriously disabling, and it is the latter group who seek treatment for their phobia.

## Treatments for anxiety

A large number of drugs have been developed in an attempt to find a satisfactory medical cure for anxiety. Many ancient herbal remedies are said to have a soothing or calming effect, and some of these are still sold and used today. Unfortunately antiquity and natural origin are no guarantee of either efficacy or safety, and there is no reason to believe that these are less harmful in long-term use than more modern medicines.

The most common of the modern tranquilizing drugs is the group of chemicals known as the benzodiazepines. This includes the well-known diazepam and nitrazepam, better known to many people under their original trade-names of Valium and Mogadon. Temazepam is another widely used member of this group, often prescribed as a sleeping tablet because of its shorter action. These have largely replaced the older drugs, of which the most important were the barbiturates, because of their greater safety, especially in overdose.

A depressingly recurrent feature in the development of psychoactive drugs is initial enthusiasm, followed by revelation of serious drawbacks to a drug or group of drugs. When a drug is first produced it is marketed, and hailed, as a significant step forward and in particular as non-addictive. Only after a period of time do its less attractive features become clear. Heroin, for example, was developed as the non-addictive alternative to morphine, yet it is now perhaps the greatest addiction problem in the world. Similarly the benzodiazepines were developed as alternatives to the highly addictive barbiturates, and it was only after several years of use that it became apparent that, although perhaps less dangerous in other ways than barbiturates, benzodiazepines were themselves strongly addictive. Temazepam, considered a major improvement as a sleeping tablet because it acts quickly and wears off quickly, especially when sold as a liquid-filled capsule, now poses a considerable problem amongst addicts who inject the liquid intravenously.

One of the problems with benzodiazepine addiction, and the main reason why it took so long to identify, is that the symptoms are almost identical to those which led the person to take it in the first place - the symptoms of anxiety. Thus when the user tries to cut down, he or she experiences withdrawal symptoms, which are

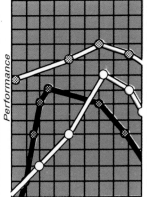

Performance

Stress or pressure

*Yerkes-Dodson curve alters according to the type of task. In each case stress initially stimulates performance, but if the stress increases, performance begins to drop. During an easy task (top curve) the stress has little effect on performance. An ordinary task (white curve) shows the classic curve, but the performance of a complex task (black curve) is greatly increased by stress at first but efficiency drops off more rapidly.*

misinerpreted as a recurrence of the anxiety. This provides evidence that they are still necessary, and so he or she continues to take them. This might not be harmful if it were not that in long-term use these drugs can produce a continuous state of mental slowing and even evidence of brain damage. Particularly in the elderly, the drowsiness and unsteadiness which they cause can result in falls and mental confusion.

The only way out of this vicious circle seems to be slow, gradual withdrawal over a long period, under close medical supervision. Attempts to cut down too rapidly, or to 'just take one when I really need them' do more harm than good.

Having said all these negative things about them, there is no doubt that in severe anxiety a short course of a benzodiazepine can be of considerable value, particularly if the cause for the anxiety is sudden and serious. Some people become so anxious in response to a serious stress in their lives that they are unable to take any effective action to deal with it. In such cases a short course of a long-acting tranquilizer such as diazepam for a week or two will lower their background level of anxiety sufficiently to be able to cope and deal with the crisis. Similarly if the anxiety is so severe as to disrupt sleep, which in turn makes it impossible to do anything to sort out difficulties the next day, then a short-acting sedative such as temazepam can be very useful for a few days.

## Beta-blockers

Although drugs acting directly on the brain are unsatisfactory, anxiety can in some cases be ameliorated by drugs which affect the nervous system in another way. The beta-blockers decrease or abolish the activity of the sympathetic nervous system. As already described, this part of the nervous system outside the brain is responsible for many of the physical symptoms of anxiety. Blocking this activity with these drugs stops the rapid pulse, the sweating and some of the symptoms in the stomach which are related to anxiety. Unlike the other drugs discussed, these are not addictive, and they act not on the brain but at the ends of the nerves scattered all over the body.

As one might expect they are particularly helpful for those who suffer primarily from the physical symptoms of anxiety, and can alleviate panic attacks. They also influence  mental anxiety indirectly, since part of the cause of  mental anxiety is the awareness of the physical changes it produces. They are nevertheless not helpful to everyone, and in few cases do they remove anxiety completely.

## Behavioral approaches to anxiety

Although drugs are of limited use in dealing with anxiety, fortunately there are alternatives. The simplest of these, which in one way or another plays a part in all treatments for anxiety, is to reduce the general level of arousal which underlies the anxiety and is produced by it. In a crude way this is what the use of beta-blockers in anxiety is intended to achieve.

A simple way to do this without drugs is by some form of relaxation exercise, in which the changes of increased sympathetic activity are consciously reversed. There are a large number of methods of relaxation training, and there is no clear evidence that any one is better in general than another, although clearly some individuals find a particular method easier. All of them include one or more of the three main aspects of relaxation: breathing, muscular relaxation and mental calming.

Although usually unconscious, breathing changes markedly according to our activity and our mood. In sleep and relaxation breathing is slow and comes from the stomach, although it is not particularly deep. The breath as it were just ebbs and flows into the body, seemingly without effort. In contrast in high levels of activity breathing is rapid and gasping, with much activity of the chest and shoulder muscles. A feature of anxiety is the use of a pattern of respiration at rest which is more suited to the athletic track. Most people can learn to control their breathing by conscious effort, and once learnt this self-control can be used to control anxiety.

For those prone to panic attacks, a more extreme method of breathing control is sometimes needed. The washing out of carbon dioxide by over-breathing which produces many of the symptoms of panic and hyperventilation can be reversed by rebreathing the air which has just been breathed out. This increases the concentration of carbon dioxide in it, and breathing this air with a larger amount of carbon dioxide reverses some of the changes in the body which cause the symptoms of panic. An easy way to do this is to place a paper bag over the nose and mouth and breathe in and out of this. Once the technique has been learnt, a paper bag can easily be carried in situations where panic is likely to occur, and used when symptoms begin.

Muscular relaxation is the second approach to relaxation. Almost always when someone is anxious their muscles tension is increased - indeed we often describe someone as tense as a synonym for anxious. Although the technique is for many people harder than the control of breathing, muscular tension too can be reversed consciously. One common method of doing this is first to contract the muscle deliberately even further, and then to relax it. Other methods include imagining that the muscles are heavy or paralysed. Part of the benefit of exercise in stress is because the increased physical activity is followed by muscular relaxation.

## Mental relaxation

In anxiety, the mind flits from one topic to another and arousing, intrusive thought about the object of concern repeatedly runs through consciousness. The use of mental images to control this excessive and over-arousing mental activity is an ancient and widespread practice. In this type of relaxation the distinction between relaxation and meditation, and between science and religion, becomes blurred.

There are a wide variety of techniques available but they all share common features. The unwanted mental activity is deliberately driven out by replacing it with a soothing mental image. This can be a visual image, such as imagining being in a quiet, relaxing place, or looking at a real or imaginary object with peaceful associations. Eastern mandelas and Christian icons are examples of the latter, but non-religious objects such as a candle flame or a flower are also often used. Another method is to imagine the mind as a turbulent pool, and then to imagine it gradually becoming a smooth, mirror-like millpond.

Auditory images are also used. The repetition of a phrase or word over and over again is used in many different systems of meditation. Such a word is known in the East as a mantra, but Christians have used a similar method in the rosary or the orthodox Anglican prayers for centuries.

A secular equivalent is to repeat the word 'Calm' or 'Peace' over and over.

These are all general methods of reducing mental anxiety. More specific ways have been developed to deal with particular anxious thoughts. These thoughts, centered on a topic which increases anxiety, in turn lead to a higher level of general arousal, and so increase anxiety still further. This in turn makes the anxious thought recur, and so the vicious circle is formed.

One way of breaking this cycle is merely to refuse to entertain the thoughts which promote anxiety. In order to do this it is important to try to identify which are the most critical types of anxious thought, and to develop ways of removing them from the mental scene.

The simplest way to counter worrying thoughts is to turn one's back on them, as it were. Part of the effect of the mantras or visual images described above is that they distract from worrying thoughts. Other methods of distraction can also be used. Counting, reciting poetry to oneself, concentrating on the things around one are all methods used to avoid anxious thoughts. 'Escapism' - gripping films, books or television shows - is a commonly used form of distraction from anxiety, although its efficacy is variable.

Another method is not to ignore the worrying thought but actively to challenge it. This has a great deal in common with the rational emotive therapy described in the previous chapter. It can be challenged either by rational argument, or merely by a strongly proposed counter-affirmation, that there is no need to worry.

## Treating phobias

Powerful irrational fears of specific situations are usually maintained by a process of avoidance; the person experiences mild anxiety on approaching the feared situation or even thinking about it, and rapidly turns in the opposite direction. This reduces the anxiety, which encourages this coping mechanism, but fails to remove the fear. In contrast if the feared situation is faced and overcome, then the fear diminishes and is eventually abolished.

There are two main methods of doing this. One is to get into the feared situation and just stay there until the fear is overcome. This is known as flooding. Although effective, it is extremely unpleasant and is not acceptable to most sufferers. A milder form of treatment to achieve the same end is systematic desensitization. The person with the fear constructs with the help of a therapist a hierarchy of degrees of fearful situation, from one promoting mild unease to sheer terror. For example someone with a dog phobia might put at the bottom of the list being close to a King Charles spaniel, with the owner present and the dog on a lead. At the top would be incarceration with an unleashed rotweiler. Other situations (a St Bernard, or a terrier) might occupy intermediate positions. The precise nature and order of the feared situations will be different for every individual.

Treatment consists of exposing the person to each situation in turn, working up the list from the least to the most feared. The person stays in the situation, doing relaxation exercises and keeping fear under control, until such time as he or she is quite comfortable in it, and then moves on to the next, until the treatment goal is reached. There may not of course be total ease in every situation; it would be foolish as well as impossible, for example, to aim for a state of total calm when locked in a room with a savage Alsatian.

With mild or simple phobias some people can overcome them without help using these basic principles; more difficult cases require professional help.

# Depression

This is the other common form of mental stress. Whereas anxiety is usually caused by uncertainty, depression is typically precipitated by loss. This may be bereavement, loss of a job or the end of a relationship, or the cause may be obscure. Some people seem unduly prone to depression, just as others are to anxiety, and get regular bouts for no apparent cause. The symptoms and treatment are rather different, although many people suffer from a mixture of the two.

Like anxiety, depression has both physical and mental symptoms. Sleep is disturbed, but whereas in anxiety the problem is in getting to sleep, people who are depressed typically wake up early - often around three a.m., and are unable to get back to sleep. Tiredness is also common, but tiredness can also cause depression, and so it is sometimes hard to decide which is cause and which is effect. Constipation is often found in more severe cases.

Like anxiety, depression may masquerade as physical illness, but depression has no physical set of changes similar to the flight or fight response of anxiety. Muscle aches, especially backache, seem to be common. It may be that depression merely makes one more aware of the physical problems of one's body, and that minor symptoms which in normal circumstances might be ignored are noticed and interpreted as signs of illness.

The most obvious and important aspect of depression, however, is its mental symptoms. These are hard to encapsulate in a single phrase, but perhaps the word negative best sums them up. Everything seems gloomy, life seems barren and hopeless, and nothing seems worthwhile. Usually sufferers see themselves as failures, often blaming themselves for their misfortunes. The depressive mood colours everything, not merely thoughts about the area of life which triggered the

## REACTIVE DEPRESSION

### FEATURES

- Sometimes referred to as neurotic depression or anxiety depression
- Often a reaction to an event such as loss of a loved one
- Stress related
- Sufferer obsessed with cause of depression
- Self-image usually remains intact
- Support from family and friends

### SYMPTOMS

- Agitation
- Anxiety
- Insomnia
- No interest in sex
- Tendency to cry
- Either loss of appetite or comfort eating

## ENDOGENOUS DEPRESSION

### FEATURES

- Usually no apparent trigger
- More likely to affect men over the age of fifty
- Chemical or hormonal changes in the body may cause it
- May occur following illness or major surgery
- Family and friends find it more difficult to be supportive

### SYMPTOMS

- Irritability
- Anxiety
- Insomnia
- No interest in sex
- Tendency to cry
- Loss of appetite
- Poor memory and short concentration time
- Low self-esteem
- Thoughts of suicide and morbid fears
- Guilt feelings
- Self neglect

depression. For example if someone becomes depressed because their marriage breaks up, nct merely may that person see himself or herself as a failure at personal relationships; other areas of life such as work or parenting also begin to look like failures also.

These negative views may even color the physical world; the weather seems more miserable, buildings more ugly, the streets dirtier. Other people seem uninterested, uncaring or perhaps unattractive and despicable. This is the result of the selective attention of depressed people, who focus on the negative. Rather than seeing the world through rose-colored spectacles, they are inclined to wear a pair with a dark grey tint.

Suicidal thoughts are common in even moderately severe depression, although attempts at suicide are rarer and indicate more serious depression.

### Treatment of depression

Depression, either mild but prolonged, or severe and shortlived, is a common reaction to stressful life events. It is important to distinguish depression which requires treatment from mere unhappiness, or a transient attack of the blues. Many people have the latter from time to time, and have their own favourite ways of dealing with it; a visit to the cinema, a good meal or a new dress or tie are popular remedies.

Even more serious depressive episodes tend to get better without treatment after a few months. But a period of several months of severe depression can literally be a living hell, and treatment which can relieve it is well worth considering.

Unlike anxiety, where the drugs available are addictive and ineffective after a short period, we have safe and effective drugs for the treatment of depression. They have a valuable place in medicine, but they too have their drawbacks. The main one is their unpleasant side-effects, which although inconvenient rather than life-threatening, are sufficiently severe to make many people unable to bear to take them. A dry mouth, blurred vision, constipation and drowsiness are the most common. These are very individual; one person may have no such effects, whilst the next may find them intolerable. Even if one drug causes severe side-effects, another may have little or none in the same person. Thus there is a considerable degree of trial and error in the choice of the drug and dosage for any individual.

Although many of these drugs are sedative, and help the sleeplessness of depression, they are not sleeping tablets in the same way as barbiturates or benzodiazepines, and they are not addictive. Unfortunately, perhaps, their biggest drawback is their delayed action. It is necessary to take an antidepressant for two or three weeks before any real benefit is felt.

## Psychological treatment

Although drugs remain the most widely available form of treatment for depression, there is now a proven effective and safe psychological treatment, known as cognitive therapy, which can help in depression. It shares as much in common with the psychological anxiety management methods discussed above.

Cognitive therapy takes the view that whatever starts depression off, it is kept going by a vicious circle process which links emotion and thought together. The depressed mood acts as a sort of filter, allowing depressing ideas through whilst keeping more positive ideas out. Depressing thoughts in turn increase the background depressed mood, which in turn makes the filter even more biased towards more depressing thoughts. Particularly important are the depressing thoughts which constantly recur and are difficult to force from the mind. This is sometimes referred to a rumination; the thought goes round and round in the mind like cud being chewed by a cow.

In cognitive therapy the sufferer learns how to reverse this process by working on the depressing thoughts. The 'filter' effect can be consciously reversed, by deliberately concentrating on more positive things, and trying to ignore or distract attention from negative thoughts and experiences. In some ways this is analogous

*A common way in which people react to stress is to use some physical substance to alleviate the symptoms. Alcohol and tobacco are the commonest in our society, but cocaine, heroin, glue and tranquilizers are increasingly widespread. Although it often appears that these have benefits in the short-term in helping the user to cope, in the longer term they are universally disastrous. They not only cause physical illnesses, since they are all more or less poisonous to the body, they also add the psychological problems of addiction to the pre-existing problems, and decrease the ability to alter situations and solve problems.*

to relaxation and distraction in anxiety, although relaxation itself is not effective as a way of combating depression; indeed it often makes it worse.

The other main technique to deal with depressing thoughts is by confrontation; again a type of rational-emotive method, where the intrusive, ruminating depressive thought is challenged and argued against logically.

Just as with anxiety management, it is possible for mild sufferers to adopt these ideas and use them on their own. Some people will find it impossible to tackle depression without outside help; particularly since a common feature of depression is inability to concentrate, lack of energy and the absence of belief in the possibility of change, or that it is worthwhile.

## Coping with stress

Although valuable, these kinds of approach to anxiety and depression are in a way locking the door after the horse has bolted. Perhaps more important is to prevent trouble by organizing one's life so as to keep stress within bounds. Of course this is not entirely possible; major tragedies and changes in life often are outside the control of the person most affected. Despite this, it is possible to take some steps to ensure the best strategies for coping with it are available.

The way we organize our lives is crucial to avoiding stress. Trying to fit too much in is a common problem. Learning to say no is an important skill to avoid a life overcrowded with commitments. Learning to say no when you want to say no, but feel you ought to say yes, is the first step. If this still does not bring life under control, then learning to say no when you want to say yes, but know you can't manage another commitment, is the next stage in the process.

Some people have the opposite problem of too few interests to stimulate them. This is particularly common in someone who has put a lot of energy into one area of life; a women with her children, typically, or a man with his job; and then the time comes when these activities come to an end. If other interests -friends, hobbies, sports and so forth - have not been developed, then the person is often lost for something to do and becomes bored and depressed. Even if only a small amount of time has been available for them, a variety of interests resembles a bud which can develop and replace the main stem of life that has been cut off. To mix metaphors, it is important not to have all one's emotional eggs in one basket.

Much stress is caused by the way that we react to people and events. It is easy to become worked up and anxious if there is too much to do, or depressed and self-pitying if we lose a job or a boy or girlfriend leaves. Building up one's mental resources to avoid being overwhelmed by these outside forces is important, and some of the techniques mentioned above can be practised in minor stresses, so that if more major problems arise they are not totally new.

There are better ways to combat stress. Exercise, recreation and holidays are all important to minimize stress. A change is a good as a rest, and a weekend of vigorous activity which contrasts with one's usual life may be as much a mental restorative as a fortnight lying semi-conscious on a beach.

Whatever your particular life and personality is like, you can benefit by analyzing the stresses upon you, seeing how you react to them and then working out ways of reducing the damage which they cause you. Studying the ideas in this section and trying them out might be one way to start this process.

# Unavoidable conditions

Whereas almost everyone has the sort of minor psychological illnesses discussed in the last chapter at some time in their lives, most of us are fortunate in being able to avoid more serious mental illness. Nevertheless such illnesses are common, compared with other important illnesses. For instance more than one in ten people will be admitted to a psychiatric ward at some time in their lives; more than will be diagnosed as diabetic. There are more beds in hospitals for psychiatric illnesses than for any other group of conditions.

These more serious illnesses can be divided into three types. Firstly there are the acute psychotic illnesses. These are in some ways similar to the conditions discussed in the last chapter. They tend to be episodic, with acute breakdowns when the sufferer becomes really quite ill, and perhaps long periods in between when he or she has no problems.

The main difference between psychotic illnesses and the illnesses discussed in the last section, sometimes referred to as neurotic illnesses, is that people who are anxious or moderately depressed are aware of their illness. They retain some insight that this is a temporary condition which is likely to pass, and that it is their perception of the situation which is part of the problem. In contrast the hall-mark of the psychotic illness is that insight into the nature of the problem is lost. Sufferers may not believe themselves to be ill at all, but blame those around them or themselves for their problems, or even deny that a problem exists.

The second type of illness is due to dysfunction of the brain, and is sometimes referred to as organic. Of course, in a sense all mental illness of whatever type is due to problems in the brain, but in organic illnesses the malfunctions in the working of the brain are more crude and obvious. A good analogy could be taken from computers. The illnesses discussed so far, both psychotic and neurotic, could be seen as due to problems with the software, whereas organic illnesses are the result of failure of the hardware. Although sometimes the distinction is obvious, in many cases the consequences are quite similar, and a considerable degree of expertise is needed to distinguish the nature of the problem (again as in computing). The most important condition of this type is dementia.

The third group of mental illnesses are the constitutional conditions. Again in a sense all mental illnesses are constitutional, since they depend to a large extent on the type of person we are and our genetic make-up. These conditions, which include mental handicap, psychopathy and what are often called personality disorders are, however, much more intimately to do with the individual than in other cases. It is much harder to separate the illness from the individual in these conditions. Consequently it is difficult to imagine what it means to see the patient without the illness, and therefore to think in terms of a cure.

These conditions will be described briefly in this chapter, together with treatments which are usually available. Although these are serious conditions, and no simple cure is available for any of them, there are approaches which can offer much relief to sufferers and to their families, both in alleviating the symptoms, and avoiding acute relapses.

## Psychotic illnesses

These are perhaps the most frightening and difficult mental illnesses, both for the sufferers and for their families and friends. Attacks may come on gradually or sometimes quite suddenly, and they can have the effect of making a pleasant and happy person severely disturbed and impossible to live with. The lack of insight may make sufferers refuse offers of help or treatment, and the major change in mental functioning may make their behavior strange, unpredictable and occasionally violent.

There has historically always been a great fear of madness, and most of the people who would popularly be called mad are in fact sufferers from psychotic illnesses. Although their strangeness and unpredictability may be frightening to those unfamiliar with such conditions, violent acts against other people are in fact rare in psychotic illness. It is because when they occur they are front-page news, which leads to a false impression, and is responsible for much of the hostility with which even in our supposedly enlightened society mental illness is viewed.

Like the minor psychological illnesses considered in the last section, these conditions arise partly as a result of an internal predisposition, and partly as a reaction to external stresses and strains. In some cultures an acute psychotic breakdown is a common reaction to stress; in this country it is rarer, except in those with an especially strong tendency to react in this way.

## Schizophrenia

This is the commonest form of psychosis, and is probably what the lay person has in mind when he or she thinks of madness, or mental illness. It is unfortunate that the term schizophrenia, which literally means split mind, has been widely confused with the phenomenon of split personality. The latter, the 'Jekyll and Hyde' situation, where one person changes character and personality completely and almost literally becomes someone else does occur, but is in fact a psychiatric rarity. Although people suffering from an acute schizophrenic illness may seem very different from their normal selves, they have not changed their personality. Like the anxious person who is 'not at all himself' different aspects may be prominent, but the sufferer is recognizably the same person.

Most psychiatrists speak of 'the schizophrenias' rather than schizophrenia, since although there are common features and a large overlap between all people suffering from schizophrenia, there are different patterns in which one or other element predominates. As in all psychological illnesses, the boundaries between different illnesses are less clear than in physical illness (where in fact it is often far from clear either). The split which is meant by the term schizophrenia is in the coherence of thought processes, and between the thoughts and the emotions. A common feature of schizophrenic illness is an inappropriate expression of emotion, or a flatness of emotion, which does not go along with the thoughts the person is having and the ideas which are being expressed. This is in contrast to depression and other 'affective' or emotional disorders, where there is a close link between thought and emotion. Indeed this link is used in treatment in cognitive therapy and anxiety management.

It seems to be in thinking that the main problems of schizophrenia lie. An important sign of schizophrenia is 'thought disorder' - a characteristic rather abnormal pattern of talking. The logical connections between one idea and the next are loose and obscure, and may be based on random factors such as rhymes or assonances in the words - sometimes referred to as 'clang' associations. The logical sequence of thought may come to an abrupt halt, and the person may suddenly stop in mid-flow. This is referred to as thought blocking. There is an imprecision in expression and a vagueness which is quite typical of the condition. Of course we are all vague, make illogical jumps of thought and associations which make sense to us but no one else from time to time. This does not make us schizophrenic. The thought problems of schizophenia are altogether more serious than these minor problems. It may of course be that the difficulties in thinking of schizophrenia are merely those which we all have, only to a more severe degree, but the result is quite different from normal illogicality, and is quite easily recognized by those familiar with it.

Probably the most common and certainly the most disturbing consequences of the thought problems suffered by people with schizophrenia are hallucinations, delusions, and paranoid ideas. Hallucinations are most often auditory, and are heard as voices talking about the sufferer, or issuing instructions. This type of hallucination is one of the causes of violence in schizophrenia, self-inflicted or against others in response to the instructions of persistent hallucinatory voices.

As well as hearing voices, sometimes people experience thoughts being put into their head, being controlled or even more alarmingly having thoughts taken out of their head. Rather than hearing voices broadcast to them alone, they may believe that their own thoughts are being broadcast for all to hear - a truly alarming prospect.

Delusions are illogical unshakable beliefs, usually false. The most common type of delusions in schizophrenia are paranoid - delusions of being persecuted. Delusions may vary from an isolated belief, perhaps related to a particular person or situation, to a complex and bizarre fantasy world, in which every action is interpreted as hostile, and the sufferer feels himself or herself to be the victim of a web of intrigue and deceit, and potentially of violence. Some experiences of the world seen through the eyes of the schizophrenic patient seem like a nightmare, and such sufferer have been described as 'the dreamer awake'.

The nature of hallucinations and delusions is very much affected by the culture to which the person affected belongs. In Western, technological society voices are often heard as radio messages broadcast for the sufferer alone. Paranoid ideas may involve spies, communists and political intrigue. In other types of society different interpretations are put on similar experiences. Where witchcraft is practised it may be a sorcerer who causes the voices to be projected to the person, and the paranoia may center on being cursed or bewitched. In religious societies voices may be believed to be supernatural, and the persecuting agent to be the devil. It is widely believed, for example, that the voices heard by Joan of Arc were a phenomenon similar to schizophrenic hallucinations.

Some people do not have the pattern of acute florid breakdowns, but nevertheless have similar symptoms, and are thought to have other varieties of schizophrenic illness. In elderly people a quieter, more chronic paranoid illness is common, sometimes with complex delusions, but sometimes with a perfectly normal mental life except in one small area. Perhaps one person or one subject will trigger off the delusions in someone who seems otherwise quite normal. The distinction between these sorts of illness and mere eccentricity can be difficult.

Another pattern may be seen, particularly in people

who have had a long succession of severe acute schizophenic illnesses. They may become withdrawn and their emotional and intellectual abilities appear to be permanently damaged. Although they may have no obvious delusional or hallucinatory symptoms, they do not return to their former selves. It is as if the trauma of their illness, and perhaps also the institutionalization and the drugs which were needed to treat it, has left them permanently scarred.

A less common but striking type of withdrawal in schizophrenia is catatonia. In the most extreme cases the sufferer is totally immobile and irresponsible, yet appears to be awake. Not only will she or he sit motionless literally for hours, but if a limb is passively moved it will stay where it is put, like a wax doll. In more mild degrees bodily movement may merely be disrupted or disorganized, almost as a physical analogy of thought disorder.

## Treatment

Until about thirty years ago there was no effective treatment for this condition, and the best that could be offered was sedation to avoid the worst effects of the experience, and custodial care in large institutions where people could be prevented from damaging themselves. A vivid and horrific description of what it felt like to undergo such an episode in those days, based on her own experiences, is given by Antonia White in *Beyond the Glass*, the last of her four autobiographical *Frost in May* novels.

There is now available a group of drugs, the phenothiazines or major tranquilizers, which although sedative in large doses, have a specific effect to suppress the abnormal thought processes which cause schizophrenia. Exactly how they do this remains unclear, but of their benefit there is little doubt. They do have some unpleasant side effects. They can cause abnormal involuntary movements and spasms, and they seem to produce a general dulling of mental activity. But against this, they can not only bring to an end the nightmare experience of an acute schizophrenic breakdown; by taking a smaller maintenance dosage it is possible to avert future episodes. Untreated, the condition tends to recur, especially in times of stress.

There is a wide variety of these drugs, and they are available in several forms. Injections or syrups are useful for emergency use, whilst tablets or long-acting injections given weekly or monthly are suitable for preventative treatment.

Psychological and psychoanalytic forms of treatment have little to offer in the treatment of schizophrenia. Psychological understanding of the disease has, however, helped to determine the best ways of supporting people with these conditions. For example, it has been shown that some people are better if they do not have too much social contact, and perhaps are better living alone than under the emotional pressures of family life. These new insights, together with the alleviating effects of the drugs, have led to new ways of caring for such people, in their own homes, or in small hostels rather than in large institutions. Admission to hospital is required nowadays for only the most serious relapses.

In many cases the person who is approaching an acute schizophrenic breakdown will realize that something is wrong. If there has been a previous episode, then familiar psychological symptoms may be recognized. Particularly if there is a clear period of stress preceding the breakdown, then the danger of 'cracking up' may be noticed, and medical help sought even in a first attack. (The majority of people who notice such symptoms are heading not for a psychotic breakdown, but a neurotic episode of severe anxiety or depression, as described in the last section.)

If help is sought early and treatment begun then it is often possible to end the period of illness quite quickly without recourse to hospital admission. Although typically insight is lost in a psychotic illness, this is not an all-or-nothing phenomenon, and many people who on the surface deny that they are ill are aware deep down that something is wrong, and with careful and sympathetic discussion will accept treatment.

Unfortunately many people do delay seeking help, or refuse treatment when it is offered. This is particularly true of someone with paranoid delusions who is quite likely to believe that the tablets or medicine offered are poisonous and to refuse them on those grounds. Sadly all too commonly is the relapse caused because someone has stopped taking their medication.

In this situation there is little that can be done, unless the person is a danger to himself or to others. There is a big difference between being mentally ill and being dangerous, even to oneself. Therefore there are many people who behave extremely oddly, and even some who are extremely distressed and unhappy because of their mental illness, who nevertheless cannot be treated unless they wish it. This is the price which has to be paid to preserve freedom of choice.

## Psychotic depression and manic-depressive illness

Depression was discussed in the last section, because it is a common condition, and the vast majority of sufferers retain insight into their mental state and realize that they are ill. Even if they cannot overcome their feelings of despair and self-hatred, they remain aware that such feelings are in fact irrational.

In a few cases of severe depression such insight is lost, and the illness becomes psychotic. The ideas of being useless or evil seen in all depressions become fixed and acquire the strength of a delusion. They may be extended to more florid expressions of self-hatred, such as a belief that the sufferer has a deserved, incurable illness, or that his or her own body is rotting. Hallucinations are rare, but they may occur. Unlike schizophrenic delusions these are tied up with guilt and feelings of self-hatred. Voices may seem to accuse them of being evil or useless.

In depression of this type the risk of suicide is high. Fortunately, sufferers respond well to drugs, although it is sometimes necessary that these be administered in hospital in order to prevent the patients talking a fatal overdose.

The timelag between starting treatment with antidepressants and their effect is discussed on pages 44-49. Because of this problem another form of treatment is sometimes used in such serious cases. Electroconvulsive therapy or ECT is sometimes also known as electric shock treatment. Although no one is quite sure how it works, the use of electrical stimulation to produce a sudden massive discharge of electrical activity in the brain has been shown to be effective in relieving depression. It acts more quickly than drugs (which is one reason for its use) and it can be effective in cases where drug treatments have failed.

The electric current passed through the brain does quite literally cause a convulsion, and the treatment was developed because it was noticed by chance that people who were depressed and who had convulsions by accident seemed to get better. In the early days the patient had an unmodified convulsion, and it was of course a horrible experience. The shock is now given with the person anesthetized, so that muscle-relaxant drugs can be used to paralyse the body temporarily, and no actual muscular spasms occur. The burst of electrical activity is restricted in its effects to the nervous system, and the person undergoing the treatment is unaware of it. Despite this it seems to many people a drastic and frightening form of treatment. Largely for this reason, it is only used in more serious cases, and is usually replaced by drug therapy when the depression is seen to improve.

Manic-depressive illness is a form of psychotic illness which seems particularly to be constitutional rather than related to outside stresses, although even so there are often external factors which trigger attacks. It is characterized by periods of profound depression, neurotic or psychotic, and other periods of the opposite extreme of emotion, hypomania. These episodes of illness are separated by periods of perfectly normal mental states which may last many years.

Manic episodes are almost exactly the opposite of depression in every sense. Instead of actions being slowed down they are speeded up. Lack of sleep and tiredness due to ceaseless activity are commonly seen. Black pessimism is replaced by an equally unrealistic optimism. Thought is again disturbed, so that grandiose plans may be made, and money spent on crazy schemes and unnecessary luxuries, because the sufferer does not stop to think. This grandiose thinking and loss of touch with reality may go so far as to cause delusions. Although in some senses hypomania is exhilarating, and may be enjoyed by the patient (though not usually by those around), this pace is exhausting, and the inability to rest and the loss of control are not always pleasant.

Sedatives are useful to control these states in the short term. A longer-acting drug which seems to have a stabilizing influence on both mania and depression is lithium. This is a salt, similar to sodium in common salt, but usually present in the body in only tiny amounts. Increasing the level of lithium in the body under careful control has been shown to be valuable not only in treating episodes of mania and depression but more importantly in preventing future attacks, which are otherwise likely.

## Organic mental illness

Perhaps surprisingly, a variety of physical illnesses produce similar changes in mental activity. A common pattern is seen whether diseases are due to an infection, a lack of blood or oxygen, or chemical imbalances in the blood, and it is not usually possible to determine the cause from the mental symptoms. This sort of illness can be divided into two types: acute confusional states which come on suddenly, and dementia which comes on more slowly, often over many years.

### Acute confusion

The name gives the most obvious features of this condition. It comes on suddenly, and lasts only as long as the illness which caused it. The most obvious feature is clouding of consciousness. The sufferer seems to be in a sort of mental 'fog' and all thought, emotion and action are impaired.

Disorientation is an easily recognizable consequence of this clouding of consciousness. The person suffering from the condition loses track of time and is not certain of where he or she is, who the people around are and loses track of time. Memory is impaired, so that familiar surroundings and people seem totally strange, and new information does not register. Someone who is confused may ask a question, receive an answer, and then ask the same question again a few minutes later.

The whole ability to think and reason is affected, but in quite a different way from the bizarre illogical jumps of schizophrenia, which seem quite sensible and obvious to the sufferer. In contrast the person who is confused seems to be groping about for meaning, trying to grab hold of thoughts, but unable quite to catch hold of them. The metaphors of 'clouding' or mental fog give a vivid picture of the nature of this phenomenon.

The metaphor of clouds is also appropriate for another feature of this condition, its tendency to fluctuate. Someone may be able to talk quite reasonably at one minute, and a few minutes later again be totally unaware of what is going on. It is not uncommon for the level of consciousness to be affected also in more severe states, and the patient to drift in and out of sleep or unconsciousness. When drowsiness or sleep occurs it is often restless, disturbed by bad dreams, and tossing and turning. People in such a state are often seen to pick at the bedclothes in an agitated manner.

The disorientation can be very frightening, and people in such states may become tearful, noisy or even violent in response to this perceived threat. The fear is sometimes made worse by the misinterpretation of things seen and heard. We have probably all had an experience such as waking in a strange room, not knowing where we are, and seeing what at first looks like a huge figure towering over us, but which on closer examination turns out to be a curtain. This seems to be the sort of misinterpretation that the confused person has, except that rather than lasting a few seconds as is usual, this illusion cannot be dismissed. In such a situation the world becomes a strange and fearsome place.

Given the correct circumstances anyone can become acutely confused, but it is more likely to happen to some people than to others. It is not uncommon for young children with high fevers to have short episodes of acute confusion, halfway between a waking confusion and a nightmare-ridden sleep. Although this is very frightening, it is not usually in fact very serious, and very high temperatures may occur in comparatively mild illnesses in children. Once the condition causing it is better then the child will return to normal.

The other group at particular risk of acute confusion are the elderly. Physiologically, young people have larger reserves to call on in times of illness. This is not so in the older person, and so it is easier for systems to fail to do their job. A chest infection, which produces fever and decreases the efficiency of the lungs (reducing the oxygen supply in the blood) can easily make the brain malfunction. This is perhaps the commonest cause. Similarly, heart failure, uncontrolled diabetes, or the failure of the kidneys or liver to work properly can have a similar effect.

## Delirium tremens

An exception to the statement made earlier that no matter what the cause, confusional states looked similar, is the reaction seen to acute withdrawal in the person heavily dependent upon alcohol. The psychological reaction to this is quite characteristic, and has its own name, delirium tremens. As well as the general characteristics of a delirious state already described, the sufferers have severe shaking, hence the 'tremens' (Latin for trembling). The most typical feature, however, is the vivid and horrific hallucinations. These have passed into popular culture as pink elephants, and although they may be as bizarre, they are rarely as benign. Horrible monsters and insects are more often seen, and may cause terror in the sufferer. A particularly unpleasant form of hallucination is 'formication' the sensation and therefore the belief that there are ants running all over the skin. The risk of convulsions and biochemical disturbances also go along with the mental symptoms, and this is therefore a potentially very serious condition which requires hospital care.

The treatment of acute confusion is to treat the cause. If, as often occurs, the underlying illness is easily alleviated, then the mental state will return to normal after a short while. Conversely, of course, if the illness cannot be cured then the outlook is grave.

# Dementia

In contrast to the rapid onset and often equally rapid disappearance of acute confusion, dementia, which shares many similar features, is usually insidious in onset and relentlessly progressive, although its progress is often so slow that the sufferer lives long enough to die of something else.

The early signs of dementia are often so subtle that they are hardly apparent except to close relatives and friends. Subtle changes in personality and minor increases in forgetfulness are common mild features. The person may notice that he or she is losing mental faculties and agility of thought. The latter realization may be deeply upsetting. Denial of the nature of the problem, both personally and to others, may provoke disputes and prevent steps to provide adequate care being taken.

As the illness becomes progressively more severe the changes become more obvious. Neglect of tidiness, cleanliness and personal hygiene is sometimes seen. As the memory goes awareness of time and space becomes confused, and disorientation, a little like that seen in the acute confusional states, may occur. Some people manage to compensate very well for these deficits, and at first sight may appear much less intellectually impaired than in fact they are. Others may become suspicious and paranoid, as they lose a clear understanding of what is going on. Other people or malign forces may be blamed for stealing things which they have in fact themselves mislaid, and so paranoid systems can be built up, although these are rarely as complex or colorful as those seen in schizophrenia.

Personality change may be marked, a previously placid person becoming aggressive and violent, whilst an assertive person may become soft and compliant. Sleep patterns may become disturbed, the person sleeping all day and being awake and restless all night - very disturbing for those living with them. Some people start to wander, setting out on an errand but forgetting where they are and where they are going. They usually end up being picked up by the police with little harm done, and can travel surprising distances, but it can be very worrying for their carers.

In the later stages the sufferer may become incontinent, not necessarily because of any physical inability, but through a lack of understanding and memory of what is required in this respect. Even self-feeding can become a problem, and intensive nursing care is needed.

There are a number of causes of dementia, all of which share the common feature of a general destruction of the brain. The two most common are cerebrovascular disease and Altzheimer's disease. The former is a disease of the blood supply, similar to that which causes heart attacks and strokes. Instead of causing the sudden death of a large amount of tissue, as happens in these conditions, the disease leads to dementia by slowly and steadily blocking off the blood supply to tiny portions of the brain so that they die.

## Altzheimer's disease

Altzheimer's disease, although symptomatically very similar, has a different appearance when the brain is examined. As well as a generalized shrinking of brain tissue commonly seen in all dementias, there are characteristic changes under the microscope. Tangles of nerve fibers are seen, distorting the normal pattern of the brain cells, and typical features known as senile plaques.

The cause of this condition is uncertain, but many causes have been suggested. A slow-acting virus, an aging process, or poisoning by aluminium are some of the theories which have been proposed.

## Other dementias

There are other rarer causes of dementia. Jacob-Creutzfelt's disease is due a slow-acting virus and is therefore thought to be infectious. The human immune-deficiency virus (HIV), the cause of AIDS, can also cause dementia. Prolonged excessive use of alcohol causes a characteristic form of dementia known as Korsakov's psychosis. In this condition people make up vivid and convincing stories to fill the gaps in their memory. The result is often fascinating and sufferers from this condition often have a lot of charm. It is easy for the unwary to be misled by their fluency into believing these 'confabulations' as they are technically known.

Although this can occur in other forms of dementia, it is more usual when the sufferers forget what is happening for them to say nothing, or admit that they do not know, or to fill in with bland and vague statements.

There are also a few reversible causes of dementia, which shade into the acute toxic confusional states discussed earlier. Deficiency of thyroid hormone, of vitamin $B_{12}$, and of folic acid (another vitamin); kidney, heart or liver failure, or diabetes are important causes of dementia, especially if it comes on suddenly. In elderly patients depression can look very like dementia. Some medications, especially tranquilizers and sedatives if taken in overdose, can cause a state closely resembling dementia. These conditions are important not because they are particularly common but because, unlike the other conditions we have discussed, they are totally treatable.

## Care of dementia

Most dementia unfortunately cannot be so easily cured, and treatment is aimed at reducing the distress experienced by the sufferers and by those who care for them. Drugs have a limited place. It is always useful to treat any physical illness which exists alongside the dementia, to ensure the person is otherwise as fit as possible.

Restlessness, especially at night, can sometimes be improved with drugs. Unfortunately many sedatives actually make confusion worse, by impairing what little mental ability the patient has left.

Behavioral techniques have been developed to help people cope with life despite mild or moderate degrees of dementia. A system known as reality orientation uses repeated reminders and obvious visual cues to help people remember where they are and what the date and time is. Large labels with words such as 'toilet', 'kitchen', 'wardrobe', on the appropriate doors can help people remember where to go and where to put things. Painting different doors and rooms different colors can also help avoid confusion. Often something will be remembered if it is said repeatedly that will not be taken in when mentioned only once.

It is possible to make the environment safer for the demented person in other ways. Kettles with automatic cut-offs can make forgetting to switch them off much less disastrous. Electric fires are safer than gas ones, which are often turned on, and then attention wanders before they are lit. Showers tend to be safer than baths, for similar reasons. Special difficult-to-open door handles are available to avoid wandering.

Help for the people, or more often one person, living with and caring for someone with dementia is vital. There are care-attendant schemes in many areas, which can provide someone to sit with the patient whilst the carer goes shopping, or merely goes out for a break to visit friends, etc. Day-centers and day hospitals provide a welcome break for both carer and patient from the monotony of everyday life, and many such patients attend these once or twice a week. Some hospitals offer holiday admissions for a week or two to give carers a longer break. Regrettably, such services are much scarcer than the need demands.

Practical help with household tasks or with meals can be provided by home-care workers, and meals-on-wheels services. This does not directly help with the care of the demented person, but it may help carers by relieving pressures in other directions, freeing their energies for their caring tasks. Nurses can visit to help with dressing and bathing.

In many areas there are support groups for people caring for a demented person. Although these groups can offer no practical help, they are most valuable in removing the feelings of isolation that are often felt by people in this position. They usually meet informally, and carers share their experiences, and learn from each other as well as from professionals such as doctors and social workers.

In a few extremely severe cases long-term hospital care is the only solution. Unfortunately, the resources available for this expensive service under the National Health Service have always been scarce, and as the pressure to contain NHS costs grows the situation becomes even more desperate.

## Personality disorder and psychopathy

There are a few people whose behaviour is bizarre and disturbed, but who do not fit any of the categories of psychological illness we have discussed so far. The term personality disorder is sometimes used to describe some of these conditions. Whether this is a medical judgement or a value judgement is debatable, and there is much debate within psychiatry about the meaning and even the value of such terms.

There do, however, seem to be some people whose whole character is such that they cannot get on satisfactorily with those around them, and their reactions to other people and to stress are destructive both to themselves and to others. They are often sad and unhappy people, who behave in ways that make it difficult to help them. Some of these behavior patterns are cleverly and amusingly described by Eric Burne in his book *Games People Play*. Much of this behavior seems to be immature and childish, as if the person concerned had never grown up. In some cases, fortunately, such people do change their behavior as they get older and become more mature in their reactions. Other undesirable patterns are ways in which most people find themselves behaving from time to time, but turned from an occasional weakness into a way of life.

A particularly important pattern of behavior of this type is sometimes referred to as psychopathy, although the term 'emotionally callous personality' used by some psychiatrists is probably a more descriptive term. The central feature of this personality type is an inability to feel guilt or to form emotional relationships with other people. They seem quite incapable of seeing things from any point of view other than their own, or of experiencing any real warmth towards another person. This leads to manipulative behavior, and on occasion to violence. Some such people are charming, but shallow and insincere; others are solitary and self-absorbed. Many of the more lurid and horrific crimes of violence which hit the headlines are committed by people who fall into this group.

Attempts to treat, in a medical way, psychopathy and other personality disorders have been largely unsuccessful. There have been a variety of experiments, usually in a residential hospital or other type of establishment, to use behavioral and psychotherapeutic methods with these sorts of problems. These have met with varying degrees of success.

## Mental handicap

It is vitally important to distinguish mental handicap from mental illness, and from the personality problems discussed above. Most sufferers from mental illness are in no way unintelligent, and except for dementia their illness does not affect their general intellectual ability. Mental handicap is in contrast a limitation on general mental, particularly intellectual, development. The majority of cases are due to congenital defects in the development of the brain, or damage occurring to it in very early life.

There is a wide variation in the severity of mental handicap. The more mild degrees shade into the lower end of the normal range of intelligence. At the other extreme there are people who never develop beyond the mental ability of an infant, and fail to learn to talk or to walk. There are, of course, all possible shades of severity in between. The more severe are often associated with physical disabilities as well, and such people often need intensive nursing care. In contrast people with mild mental handicap may in other ways be quite fit, able to look after themselves in a sheltered environment, and hold down a simple job.

At one time it was the practice to remove sufferers from mental handicap into residential hospitals, often deep in the country, and encourage their families to reject and ignore them. Although the motivation behind this policy was well-meaning, it is now felt that it is better both for the individuals concerned, and for society, for them to be cared for at home, or in small groups in homely hostels rather than in large institutions. In this way the person's maximum potential can be realized, even if this potential is severely limited.

This policy, although probably more humane, does place enormous emotional, practical and financial strains on families, and can lead to problems when elderly parents die, or become incapable of caring for their mentally handicapped offspring. Satisfactory ways of dealing with these problems are only just being developed.

## Obsessions and compulsions

Less frequent than generalized anxiety or phobias, but nevertheless not a rare phenomenon, is the obsessional-compulsive neurosis. We all act obsessionally to some degree, checking and rechecking things to make absolutely sure, even though logically we know that it is not necessary. Many of us also have more or less rational rituals which we carry out which make us feel less anxious in stressful situations. These become neurotic only when they reach a point when they interfere with everyday life, often when they are associated with an extreme anxiety state.

Some obsessive rituals are logically related to the cause of anxiety. Perhaps the commonest is hand-washing, associated with a fear of dirt or contamination. It is normal and healthy to wash one's hands when one has dealt with something dirty or potentially infectious; it is natural if not logical to wash them when one has come close to such a contact, even if not actually risked physical contamination. The problem for the obsessional hand-washer is the inability to be convinced that the hands are clean, so that they are washed over and over again until they are red and sore. Lady Macbeth was the most well-known sufferer from this complaint.

Similarly it is not uncommon to check that doors are locked at night, and then forget and check again. The obsessional, however, will stay up half the night checking. Superstitious compulsions are rather similar. Children often play a game of walking along a pavement without stepping on the cracks. For the compulsive, this will cease to be a game and be a matter of great psychological importance.

In all these cases the person with the compulsion is anxious. Carrying out the activity which the compulsion directs makes him or her less anxious. But then doubts creep in - was it done correctly? And so anxiety rises again until the ritual is performed again, and so the cycle goes on.

Behavioral treatment of this complaint is directed at stopping the person reducing the anxiety by the ritual act, and so rendering the action psychologically futile. Instead other methods such as relaxation are used to deal with the anxiety. In the same way, the phobic person must not be allowed to avoid the frightening situation. It must be faced and the fear overcome. Where uncertainty is a sustaining factor in checking, then developing the habit of one very thorough checking system can be helpful.

# Alternative treatments

## Introduction

Mental and emotional health is an area where alternative medicine has a tremendous amount to offer. The concept of treating the whole person, which is central to natural therapies, obviously involves the mental aspects of any disorder and these are inseparable from the physical side of health. Indeed, virtually all physical problems are in some way related to the mind. On the other hand, fluctuations in hormone production will lead to problems of mood, for instance in post-natal depression or premenstrual tension. Inadequate absorption of nutrients can affect the nervous system, as can a lack of oxygen through shallow breathing patterns or respiratory disorder.

It is thus not possible or appropriate to separate out mental problems from the rest of the person's health, and it is the very holistic nature of alternative medical systems which is their strength in assessing and treating the mind as part of, or indeed the cause of, illness. There are a number of such approaches, which look at the mind and disturbances in occasionally differing ways, although often with many complementary treatments - for example, manipulative treatments for a back problem may well be supported by counseling for the emotional causes producing the physical discomfort.

Mental and emotional disorders, and physical problems which directly and obviously stem from the mind, are conditions where alternative approaches have often had major benefit - due in part to the importance they attach to looking at the whole person in any illness - and there are accordingly a number of treatments which are available. Therapists may also advise self-help measures, such as relaxation classes, in conjunction with their treatment.

## Acupuncture

Traditional Chinese medicine is concerned with the maintenance of internal harmony through the movement of energy, termed Chi, around the body. Any disturbances in the flow of Chi create an imbalance which will lead to ill-health. This flow occurs along invisible pathways or channels, usually called meridians, and acupuncturists correct any distortions of such circulating Chi. Interestingly, Chinese medicine does not recognize the nervous system as it is understood in Western medicine, but sees normal functioning of all the systems as part of the role of Chi.

## Aromatherapy and/or massage

Although these are two therapies, aromatherapists in the main use massage as the form in which they treat people with aromatic essential oils, at least in this country, and so I have put them together here. The benefits of massage itself are mainly for inducing greater relaxation and improving circulation, and are very applicable to stress-related problems. Plant-based essential oils can also have profound effects on the mood (we can all associate certain smells with a memory or emotion) and when used in conjunction with massage a double effect is created.

## Chiropractic and osteopathy

Up to seventy per cent of back conditions are related to emotional or psychological problems, and so the manipulative therapists will be on the lookout for such causes, either counseling or giving advice themselves, or referring for other help alongside their treatment. It is also true that structural imbalances can lead to feelings of depression etc, or to other symptoms such as headaches, and so these therapies have a wider role than just 'back-menders'. They differ in their form of manipulation and approach, but are often thought of in the same category as they both deal with the structure of the body.

## Herbal medicine

Like other major alternative therapies, herbal medicine is concerned with treating the individual, with all the interaction between the physical, emotional and mental levels that is involved in a holistic approach - 'whole plants for whole people'. Due to the complex nature of plants, they often can have effects on the mind as well as bodily functions, helping to restore overall balance. The impact of the mind on the body, and of physical disorders on the mind, is considered very important by medical herbalists, who will use remedies and advice to support our own attempts to correct the problems.

# Homeopathy

This is based on the premise of treating 'like with like' - that is, giving a highly diluted dose of something which in large amounts would induce the same symptoms in a healthy person as those being experienced by the patient. In looking at the symptoms, the homeopath places mental and emotional problems first, because these determine the individual's personality and this is the essential basis for homeopathic prescribing. Improvements in emotional states are often the first signs that a person is recovering from an illness, mental or physical.

# Hypnotherapy

Hypnotherapists are exclusively dealing with the mind, in the sense that it is the mental attitudes and emotional imbalances that lead to disturbances in behavior or disease that are the focus for their treatment. By inducing a more receptive state of mind the hypnotherapist aims to encourage positive thought processes through suggestion and visualization, or will use this quietened state to explore past traumas and help the person analyze the root causes of their problems.

# Naturopathy

The vital importance of what we put into our bodies, whether it be the diet, drugs and toxins like tobacco or alcohol, or environmental pollution, is the key factor in naturopathic treatment. There are many studies confirming the effects of poor nutrition or chemicals on behavior and mood, even with quite severe disturbances. Apart from being a discipline in their own right, naturopathic principles underline much of other therapies' approaches to health, particularly herbal medicine.

## Psychotherapy

This is often termed the talking therapy, but there are a number of theoretical styles which come under the umbrella title of psychotherapy. There are links between them and more conventional psychiatry, but they carry less of a stigma and are often able to explore a person's problems in a less rigid format than in hospital or clinic settings. In a wider sense, counseling skills and techniques may well be employed by other alternative therapists.

## Stress

The effects of undue stress, and ways to cope with it when it is excessive or prolonged, are one of the major challenges to health-care today. Alternative medicine is well placed to meet this challenge, with its insistence on treating each person as a unique individual, with all levels of activity from physical to mental being taken into account. Some of the most influential work on stress mechanisms and our capacity to withstand pressures was done some years ago by Selye and others, and a feature that is emphasized by therapists in one way or another is our ability to maintain normal functioning as far as possible through a series of controls and feedback mechanisms - often called the principle of homeostasis. This self-balancing principle is encouraged by all the therapies discussed in this book, whether they have a physical, mental or energy-based approach.

In general, the alternative therapies see much of modern lifestyle as creating an unnecessary burden of stress on our systems. The recent increased concern with the environment and the interaction between us and the natural world is one that has occupied the therapists' attention for some time - for instance herbalism is green medicine in more ways than one - and most of the treatments will involve advice on how to adapt our lifestyle to achieve greater harmony and reduction of stress factors.

Thus, not only will the practitioner aim to improve the person's ability to cope with a stressful situation but also he or she will be looking to ensure that there is less self-induced stress around. For each therapy there is a different, although often complementary, approach.

In acupuncture, the flow and distribution of Chi is paramount, and treatment will be aimed at strengthening weaknesses in energy lines, or meridians. The functioning of the mind is linked to the functioning of our internal organs, and the acupuncturist balances these through the meridian pathways which energize our body. Massage, whether used as part of aromatherapy or on its own, is intended primarily to achieve greater relaxation and so lessen the effects of stress. By becoming more relaxed in general, people often adopt a more easy-going attitude to the problems and so learn to manage stress levels better.

Herbal medicine has a range of remedies which can be of benefit. Many herbs have a calming effect, from the gentle relaxants to those with more sedating properties; a different class of remedies are those which are nervous restoratives, helping to nourish and build up the nervous system after prolonged stress; and a third important group are the adaptogens, which act in a complex way to help the body adapt to stress, improve stamina and so on - Ginseng is the most well-known example of this type of medicine. Homeopathy is most concerned with the individual's reactions and response to the stress, since it is the emotional state and behavior which determines the appropriate remedy. When homeopathic medicines were first being tested, or 'proved', it was these mental and emotional differences that were the most noticeable symptoms and that led to the remedy picture. Therefore, although they will be concerned with reducing the stresses themselves, homeopaths concentrate more on the way in which the person is reacting to them.

For the naturopath, one of the main aims is to strengthen the ability of the individual to withstand external pressures, whilst ensuring that the nervous system is adequately nourished and supplied with blood and oxygen to function as well as possible. Through the diet, or with supplements, the correct amounts of vitamins and minerals are given, and also advice on exercise and relaxation to keep the mind and body in peak condition.

Hypnotherapy and psychotherapy use a variety of techniques to help the person bring out underlying worries that are contributing to the stress levels, and also use relaxation exercises, tapes and so forth in order to calm the mind and aid the person to sort out the problems and so deal with the stress better. Often therapists nowadays run stress management courses or packages for this very purpose, recognizing that for many people high levels of stress are an everyday part of their lives.

Some find that prolonged stress leads to increased strain on the body, with muscular or even structural problems developing, and it is with these latter that the manipulative therapies will be helpful. Osteopaths and chiropractors recognize the psychological component in the majority of skeletal disorders, and will often give advice or refer for additional help with this, but they can give tremendous relief from the physical discomfort itself. This in turn releases energy, which improves mobility and creates better physical conditions for coping with the stress. In addition to the treatments themselves, many of the above therapists will also advocate that people look at ways to help themselves. For instance, relaxing exercises such as yoga or t'ai chi can be very beneficial - indeed, increasing exercise and physical stamina generally often helps to increase ability to cope with mental stress. The regular practice of meditation has been shown to have a marked effect on stress symptoms like high blood pressure. Postural and occupational strains on the body can also be alleviated, for example by lessons in the Alexander Technique to learn more efficient ways to use our bodies. All these approaches can fit in very well with alternative treatments, and are often incorporated into the overall program by the therapist.

# Depression

There is a tremendous difference between the occasional low feeling that we all experience and clinical depression. The latter is a deep-rooted condition which often requires working on several aspects of lifestyle, and the depressed person is typically not at all motivated to do anything to help. This applies whether the depression is reactive (i.e. the depression is a reaction to some external event in life) or endogenous. In traditional terms, depression was seen as a condition resulting from excess black bile, producing melancholia, and treatment was often aimed at the liver. This is an important consideration, since digestive and liver function can play a large part in creating or alleviating depression, especially where alcohol or drugs are involved.

In acupuncture, this view is echoed by the association of depression with a stagnation of liver Chi. This in turn can be related to repressed feelings, especially of anger, and the treatment would focus on moving and stimulating the Chi. As with many of the other therapies, acupuncturists may well suggest counseling to help the person deal with the repressed or blocked emotions.

Like acupuncture, herbal medicine has a long tradition of treating people with depression, and of looking at the wider aspects of the condition. There may be an emphasis on the diet, including reducing the intake of alcohol and so on, and improving liver function will again be part of the treatment plan. In addition, the herbal practitioner will be likely to prescribe nervous restoratives to slowly but steadily assist the return to normal functioning - an example might be St John's Wort (*Hypericum perforatum*) which exerts a genuinely anti-depressant action over a period of several weeks. Many traditional remedies for depression were plants which act as bitters, stimulating tonics to the digestive and liver function; indeed the herbal *materia medica* is rich in 'tonics' to encourage better physical and mental activity.

Naturopathic treatment will also pay great attention to the correct nutritional balance, both with the view of avoiding harmful substances and of supplementing the diet to provide sufficient vitamins and minerals; the importance of the vitamin B complex for the nervous system is an example. Many naturopaths are also osteopaths, and these and other manipulative therapists can help to sort out spinal rigidity and tension which can contribute to the overall problems linked to the depression. Such areas of physical tension, this time affecting the muscles, can be relieved by regular massage, which has the additional benefit of being pleasant and not demanding too much from the person. For deeper effects on the mood, this can then be incorporated into aromatherapy treatment, since the aromatic essential oils have profound effects on how we feel towards some people.

Homeopaths will determine the precise way in which patients are displaying their feelings of depression, or are reacting to some traumatic event, and they will prescribe on this basis. This can often act in a subtle way to shift the central cause of imbalance - that is the disturbance in the personality and temperament.

Central to any successful treatment program is counseling, and here the use of psychotherapy is a major factor. This will be aimed at any external stresses or traumas which have occurred, either immediately prior to the state of depression or earlier in life, and which the person has been unable to cope with or to release. Also, the counseling will help individuals to gain a clearer perspective on their own feelings and responses, and to make some positive move to regain self-confidence and esteem. Hypnotherapy can help significantly in these areas, both by applying the analytical skills of counseling and also by harnessing the capacity for emotional release and positive thought that the hypnotic state brings about.

Depression, and its counterpart, anxiety which often accompanies or precedes it, is a condition for which there are therefore a number of therapeutic approaches. These are in many cases complementary to each other, especially in the use of counseling, and provide real alternatives to the conventional treatment by anti-depressants. The latter is particularly limited in its effectiveness against depression stemming from external causes. The emphasis of the natural therapies is to support the sufferer from depression from within. The problem that all therapists may well face, however, is to maintain the cooperation and motivation of the patient.

One especial situation that can provoke great depression is when somebody reaches the point of nervous breakdown. This is when the mental, emotional and finally physical overload is so great that the person completely ceases to cope. The approach of the natural therapies is in essence the same as for stress conditions generally, but since the anxiety or depression is so acute and usually accompanied by complete prostration the treatment needs to be more intense. This can require complementary approaches, using the counseling skills of psychotherapy or hypnotherapy alongside treatments such as acupuncture, herbal medicine or homeopath.

## Psychosomatic illness

The interrelationship of the mind and the body is an essential aspect of alternative medicine, and this is most obviously seen in psychosomatic illness. The effects of acute mental distress, such as bereavement, on physical health are perhaps the most marked example. Changes in heart rate and rhythm, blood pressure, appetite, digestion and physical appearance can occur very quickly. It is in the longer term, however, that such shock can have the most serious effects. This also applies to chronic mental stress or disturbance, which is a significant factor in many illnesses ranging from gastric ulcer or irritable bowel syndrome to the development of cancer.

Some specific examples of psychosomatic disorders are covered in other sections of this book, so here it is more the general principle that is important. Because the alternative therapies lay greater emphasis on the treatment of the whole person, they are more likely to take account of and be able to deal with the psychosomatic element of ill-health. Each therapy has its own strategy and therapeutic tools to help treat the mental and emotional causes of physical illness.

For herbal medicine, the range of applicable remedies is wide, covering those with relaxant or even sedative properties, stimulants to the central nervous system, tonics and nervous restoratives; the choice for any individual will depend on the circumstances, and may vary over time. These are backed up by remedies which deal with the physical manifestations of the stress, so that herbal medicine is able to treat the symptoms as well as the cause - the latter naturally have a higher priority for full restoration of health.

Since homeopathy looks first at the personality and mental characteristics of each patient, it will very obviously be concerned with these causes of illness and treatment is aimed more at them than at the physical symptoms. The goal in homeopathic prescribing is to determine the constitutional remedy i.e.. the remedy which is applicable to the background mental and emotional make-up of the individual; in psychosomatic illness this would thus be used first, to restore balance.

In acupuncture, the fundamental imbalances in energy flow are the key to all illness, and the mind is linked to this flow along the pathways or meridians. Consequently, by restoring balance in the distribution of energy, or Chi, both the mental pressures on the body and the physical disorder itself can be corrected.

With back problems in particular osteopaths and chiropractors are very aware of the power of mind over matter. Their treatments are directed mainly at the structural problems, but counseling and advice on the mental or emotional aspects is a frequent part of their overall approach. Some specific forms of treatment, especially cranial osteopathy, are in fact aimed more at the underlying energy blockages and have profound effects on the mental level as well as the physical lesion.

It is in the area of psychosomatic illness that the hypnotherapy and psychotherapy practitioners play a large role. We have already dealt with their skills in helping to understand inner turmoil and in stress management; these are of great value in sorting out the cause of the physical problem and altering the attitude of the patient so that positive healing energy can be focused from within, rather than the negative, destructive mental state which helped create the illness. So often it is the holding on to negative emotions, reflecting them inwards, that is the foundation of the condition, and these therapies can help the person to free patients of such feelings.

Since a great deal of psychosomatic illness is a result of excessive stress, all that has been said in that context is likely to be applicable. Certainly, the benefits of aromatherapy, massage and the relaxation disciplines such as yoga or meditation in calming the individual's stress are considerable, and encourage self-healing to take place.

# Insomnia

The biggest factor in producing insomnia is anxiety or worry, and any successful treatment needs to provide support and help with these underlying problems. Conventional sleeping pills are clearly not to be recommended in this context, and their tendency to be addictive makes their use less preferable to other treatments. Lack of sleep over time will itself cause mental and physical distress, but it is most frequently the case that worry, restlessness and so forth is the original fuel that starts the vicious circle. Each practitioner will therefore attempt to determine what these anxieties are and to help with their resolution, as well as treating the person directly.

Naturopaths approach the problem by transferring attention from sleep to health. Anxiety and restlessness show up in other areas of lifestyle, including eating habits, irritability and so on. The importance of nutrition is central to naturopathy, and if this is disturbed then the sleep center in the brain will be affected. Dietary factors will affect sleep patterns in other ways; indigestion is itself a frequent cause of insomnia. The intake of stimulants such as coffee or high-protein foods in the evening create extra brain activity, while foods rich in calcium and magnesium have a relaxing effect.

There can be great benefits in soft-tissue massage, especially at the base of the head and the neck. This improves circulation, allowing the congestion in the cranium to disperse, and also gives greater relaxation. The use of suitably relaxing essential oils, such as lavender, rose, marjoram and so on, will definitely add to these benefits. One of the problems for long-term insomniacs is to relearn the art of relaxing, and massage is a good first step in this direction. This could be backed up by exercises for releasing muscle tension, and classes in yoga are very helpful. Traditional Chinese medicine sees insomnia as a disturbance of the Shen or 'spirit'. This in turn is often related to a deficiency of the blood Chi, affecting the heart and perhaps the liver meridians. This underlying blood deficiency is often strengthened by Chinese herbal tonics, alongside the acupuncture treatment. As with other therapies, acupuncturists may well suggest counseling if there are deeper emotional difficulties leading to the lack of sleep.

Herbal medicine is aimed at supporting the person to regain a natural sleep pattern, rather than sedation, and so prescriptions will emphasize nervous restoratives such as wild oats (*Avena sativa*) or skullcap (*Scutellaria lateriflora*) which help to calm without a 'knockout' effect, for long-term strengthening and nourishing. More strongly acting relaxants like cowslips (*Primula veris*) may of course be needed in the first instance. In addition, herbalists will see what steps people can take themselves to change the cycle of insomnia, irritability and over-tiredness. The individual pattern of behavior that leads to this cycle is the province of the homeopath. For instance, the remedy Sepia might be applicable to someone who is normally active but is easily tired or gets run down and irritable, finds noise very disturbing for sleep and difficulty in going back off to sleep once awake, feels that everyday life is a great burden, whilst needing to have some framework and direction to life and self-compelled to fulfil this. If this pattern of behavior was clear enough, then a single dose of the remedy, at a high dilution, would be prescribed to restore harmony and thus sleep.

Manipulation can also play a role for some insomnia-related problems. For instance, the tendency to teeth-grinding can stem from a misalignment of the jaw, or circulatory congestion may come from a rigidity of the cranial bones, and in both cases the symptoms can lead to disturbed sleep. Quite clearly, the most prominent reasons for insomnia are worries and anxiety, and these need to be addressed for real change in sleeping patterns to be made. The help of hypnotherapy in this respect is valuable, with therapists using the hypnotic state to make it easier for someone to bring out problems from subconsciousness and to explore ways to resolve them.

Something that is often overlooked is that insomnia can frequently result from a state of depression or over-tiredness, rather than excess tension. For these people especially the prescribing of sleeping pills is counter-productive, simple adding to the underlying depression. In any event, the potential for addiction, as well as depression, of such medication makes the options described above highly preferable forms of treatment.

## Headache and migraine

Headaches are caused by a great number of factors, both physical and psychological. Examples of these are: tension, depression, indigestion, high blood pressure, low blood-sugar levels (hypoglycemia), excessive amounts of noise, changes in atmospheric pressure, dietary factors, eye strain and more. It is thus vital that persistent or repetitive bouts of headache in particular are investigated thoroughly for the individual cause involved.

As far as migraines are concerned, the complexity and variety of triggers are probably even greater. There is certainly a family tendency, although this may simply reflect a similar lifestyle. The most significant factor is stress, with the migraine symptoms appearing at times of increased pressure, or perhaps when the stress eases off - for instance the quite common pattern of weekend migraine. Other triggers include certain foods, noises, aromas, flashing lights and hormonal fluctuations and so forth, and there can frequently be a structural or postural ingredient in the condition. All this means that a person who suffers from migraine should keep looking at treatment choices to find help, rather than 'learning to live with it' as is sometimes suggested.

For medical herbalists, apart from the obvious need to closely investigate the causes for the headache, the pattern of migrainous conditions falls into two broad groups; these are termed 'hot' or 'cold' migraines. This traditional distinction relates to whether there is respectively excessive vasodilation (expansion and engorgement of the blood vessels of the head), or intense vasoconstriction. For sufferers of the first kind the use of ice-cold applications is often helpful, while the latter group will benefit from hot packs.

There are many herbal remedies of long-established value for migraine sufferers - for instance rosemary (*Rosmarinus officinalis*) which improves digestive and liver function (often a contributory factor) and relaxes the constricted blood vessels. A recently popular herb, feverfew (*Chrysanthemum parthenium*), acts in a similar way and is thus particularly valuable for the 'cold' type of migraine. Also of concern to the herbalist, and central to naturopathic advice, is the role of any dietary factors. Common triggers are alcohol (especially red wine) chocolate, cheese, eggs and so on. Apart from these direct connections, naturopathic treatment will look at the role of the digestive system in general (what are called stomach migraines, or liverish headaches) and through this the health of the blood supply to the cranium.

Chiropractic or osteopathic treatment is frequently called for in the management of migraine or recurrent headaches, particularly where there is pain and/or stiffness in the neck. Restrictions in the cervical vertebrae in the neck, even extending down to the thoracic region, will produce muscle spasm and affect the circulation to the head, and manipulative correction will benefit greatly.

Such work may be accompanied by soft-tissue treatment, and using massage to loosen tight muscles will be highly valuable; this can be helpful in the earliest stages of such a migraine pattern, but is probably best as a course in between actual attacks to prevent recurrence. Tension headaches are also well-treated in this way. Using locally vasodilator essential oils, such as rosemary or lavender, will improve the results during a migraine stemming from neck muscle spasm.

In acupuncture, the different patterns of migraine headaches are seen as excessive liver Chi rising to the head, or as blood deficiency. One of the key concepts in Chinese medicine is that of yin/yang, the opposing yet balanced forces that lie behind all life. Examples are light/dark, hot/cold, expansion/contraction etc. The normal movement of liver Chi is due to its yang nature, that is upward and outwards. If this is blocked, e.g. by stress, alcohol, fatty foods and so on, then the build up of Chi rises and causes the pressure and pain in the head; reactions in energy flows mean that the stomach Chi creates nausea and/or vomiting. Treatments to balance the energy flow are thus the means to restore harmony and to stop the migraines.

Homeopathy is rich in remedies which contain headaches as part of their symptom-picture, and so the great art is the establishment of the correct remedy for the individual. The precise nature and pattern of the ache is vital for diagnosis; when the pains come on or are aggravated or improved, any other sensitivities such as noises, smells, etc and especially the person's reactions to the condition and general personality - all these go to build up the appropriate jigsaw that leads to the right treatment.

For all these therapies, the importance of assessing the individual lifestyle is included in treatment. For instance, the use of the contraceptive pill is almost always an aggravating factor; diet, exercise and posture are equally significant areas for evaluation. The role of stress, especially sudden stress release, has already been mentioned and counseling or hypnotherapy skills can help here. The major thing to note is that there are good choices for positive help from natural medicine.

## Alcoholism and addictions

Dependence on alcohol, or indeed a number of drugs, brings in a whole series of interrelated factors; there are physiological and chemical changes that occur in response to the alcohol, strong emotional and psychological effects from it and reasons for becoming or staying alcoholic, and widespread social implications. Therefore successful help for alcoholics and other addicts needs to address all these areas.

It is clear that individual therapies cannot offer assistance in all the aspects of the problem, and complementary work may involve several agencies. One of the greatest needs for alcoholics who break the habit is an ongoing support network, to encourage, advise and reshape their life-direction: the most obvious is Alcoholics Anonymous who specialize in counseling and group support in this area. Nowadays they are being contacted more and more by addicts of other drugs as well, and help follows similar lines.Each addictive drug has its own particular effects, and social pressures may depend on how acceptable or legal the substance is, but the approaches discussed here will have general applications for addicts. The old vexed question of whether alcoholics are born or made is not of real relevance with individual-based treatments, but the consensus is that an addictive personality can be perceived. With drugs that are prescribed, such as the tranquillizers, this is less significant than the biochemical effects which take place.

Acupuncture has a good track record for the treatment of dependency patterns - for example cigarette smokers, heroin users and so on - and relates the physical and emotional imbalances to energy distribution. Alcohol is seen to create damp heat, especially in the liver and spleen channels, and treatment would focus on dispersing the stagnant Chi and reducing the heat.

The liver is also the key organ for herbal treatment, and remedies to detoxify and repair damage to it are the prime treatment. Good examples of mild liver tonics are milk thistle (*Carduus marianus*) and dandelion (*Taraxacum officinalis*); over time these help to restore liver function as far as possible, and this in turn has benefits for the whole person.

The personality aspects are likely to determine homeopathic prescribing; for instance, if the person feels trapped in life and wishes to avoid responsibility, then the remedy Lycopodium may be given. For all three therapies, the need for counseling to assist the alcoholic is crucial, and psychotherapy or hypnotherapy may be recommended alongside their treatments.

The anxiety and stress that contributes to alcohol dependence, and certainly will accompany withdrawal, is an aspect that the counsellors will address. Of great benefit here also is massage, particularly of the abdomen and back, which stimulates circulation and internal organ function as well as aiding relaxation. For the aromatherapist, the use of oils which increase elimination and detoxification, such as juniper and fennel, is added to the massage effects. One of the saddest things about withdrawal from alcohol or other drugs is the degree of poisoning symptoms that the person has to suffer before trying to rebuild life without the prop. This is particularly true of the benzodiazepines, the family of so-called minor tranquillizers which includes Valium and Ativan for example. Whilst alcohol can be physically very damaging, and heroin withdrawal is traumatic in its reactions, withdrawal symptoms from these tranquilizers involve physical and psychological disturbances that can last for months, if not years.

Helping to cope with all these reactions is an important role for the natural therapies, and their gentler approaches are well suited to this task. For the person dependent on alcohol or other drugs the best policy is probably to adopt a range of strategies, both conventional and alternative, that will give the greatest support to attempts to come off and stay off the drug.

## Hormonal effects on the mind

Just as the mind can affect our physical processes, including the operation of the endocrine glands, so in turn any disturbances in the hormone production by the latter will affect our mental and emotional state. Examples are the interrelationship between chronic stress and the adrenal glands, the tiredness and mental confusion that accompanies an underactive thyroid or the anxiety and panicky feelings of thyroid overactivity, the aggression and irritability of diabetic states and so forth.

Two specific examples that are very common and illustrate some alternatives to conventional treatment are premenstrual tension and menopausal irritability and depression. The use of hormone replacement therapy for menopausal women is increasing rapidly in this country; while it can offer benefits in the short term for many women, it is not without risks and is essentially attempting to hold back the changes that are a part of the natural aging process. The aim of alternative medicine is to support the woman as she goes through these changes. Similarly, for symptoms associated with PMT, treatment is intended to restore a natural balance rather than administering synthetic hormones or just sedating.

The naturopath focuses on nutrition and circulation.. In the case of PMT, supplementation of the diet with nutrients like vitamin $B_6$, magnesium and calcium can reduce some of the symptoms very effectively; menopausal imbalances may require the vitamin B complex for nerve functioning, calcium (with magnesium and vitamins A and D) to slow the tendency towards osteoporosis. Exercises and the use of hot and cold packs will improve pelvic circulation and lessen fluid retention that adds to the pressure and tension felt premenstrually.

Herbal medicine is rich in plants that influence our hormone production - the prime example for PMT is the herb chaste tree (*Vitex agnus-castus*), which encourages the corpus luteum to function properly and produce sufficient progesterone during the second half of the menstrual cycle. Lack of this hormone creates most of the physical and mental difficulties pre-period. Herbalists will also treat the anxiety, depression and irritability directly, with relaxing remedies such as chamomile or nervous restoratives.These latter remedies are also of great value during the menopause, to alleviate the mental fatigue and sensitivity that often occurs, alongside tonics for the ovaries etc. At this time, exercise is very useful to slow down calcium loss and to reduce tension: the practice of yoga is often recommended. Massage is an excellent way of relaxing the person, improving the circulation, enhancing skin tone, and releasing fluid from the tissues. Consequently, it works very well for women suffering either of these two problems, on its own or in conjunction with other therapy. Since the pelvic basin acts to pool and congest the circulation, drainage is important to relieve the physical discomfort, but this will also help with the mental imbalance by encouraging a better blood flow and nutrient supply to the brain. In their own ways, homeopathy and acupuncture address the underlying fundamental imbalances that produce the reactions in the mind and body to hormone upsets; homeopaths in particular are more concerned with the individual's characteristic personality than the physical changes leading to the tension. As an illustration, the remedy Pulsatilla is suited to women of a gentle and affectionate nature who are prone to bursting into tears - this is applicable for a wide range of health problems, given their basic constitution.

Another related condition is that of post-natal depression, sometimes known as the 'baby blues'. The complete change in lifestyle that is brought about by parenthood is in itself often a trigger for an emotional downswing after the childbirth, and the usual disruption in sleeping patterns is not helpful in this respect. Of major significance, however, is the alteration in hormone levels, especially the drop in progesterone that occurs some weeks after childbirth. The approaches mentioned above - e.g. herbal medication - are also of great value here, probably with even more discussion and advice on how to cope with the changes. Although the counseling therapies have a role in helping the person to come to terms with and resolve some of the emotional problems that can arise with these conditions, especially the post-natal problems, it is likely that the more physical-based systems discussed above will be central treatments.

## Phobias, manias, personality disorders

This heading covers a wide range of conditions, ranging from mildly neurotic states to obsessions, delusions, paranoia etc., many of which will in conventional medicine be treated by psychiatric and/or strong drug approaches. It would be foolish to suggest that all neuroses or psychoses can be easily treated by other means, but there are possibilities of help for a number of people in these categories. One stumbling block can be the need for continued support and care at home.The hypnotherapist offers a different approach to usual counseling, and is often able to retrace the development of say a phobia back to an experience earlier in life. By bringing this in to the conscious mind it can be put into perspective and becomes less threatening or disabling.

Both homeopathy and acupuncture will treat the person constitutionally, working with the vital force or energy in their own ways, and it is thus difficult to be specific about the nature of the treatments. It is fair to say that homeopathic treatment in particular may be hampered by the use of powerful conventional drugs.

Medical herbalists can achieve a good deal through relaxants and remedies to restore a debilitated nervous system, such as oats, ginseng and vervain. Traditional medicine would in the past have involved the more psychoactive plants, as part of a healing ritual to fully 'cleanse' the mind and soul. This is a neglected aspect of medicine, which might repay careful study.

Each therapy in its own way has something to offer, since symptoms often mirror everyday stress reactions, but with greater insensitivity and frequency. Conditions like schizophrenia for instance have been shown to be amenable to dietary treatments, aromatherapy oils have pronounced effects on the mood, e.g. clary sage has a euphoric effect not unlike a mild cannabis reaction, in China acupuncture is used for serious mental disorders, so the potential is there. At the same time, it is important to sound a note of caution, especially when looking at severe mental disturbances such as the schizophrenic disorders, since the scope for benefit by natural methods may be quite limited and there is not the back-up of the resources available through conventional medicine.

## Other titles in the series

Your Active Body (ISBN 0 245-55070-4)
Your Sex Life (ISBN 0 245-55067-4)
Your Heart and Lungs (ISBN 0 245-55069-0)
Your Pregnancy and Childbirth (ISBN 0 245-55068-2)
Your Mind (ISBN 0 245-60008-6)
Your Diet (ISBN 0 245-60009-4)
Your Skin (ISBN 0 245-60010-8)
Your Child (ISBN 0 245-60011-6)

**Available, Autumn 1990**
Your Female Body (ISBN 0 245-60012-4)
Your Senses (ISBN 0 245-60013-2)
A-Z of Conditions and Drugs (ISBN 0 245-60014-0)

## Useful organizations

The National Association for
Mental Health (MIND)
22 Harley Street
London W1N 2ED

MENCAP
123 Golden Lane
London EC17 0RT

Relaxation for Living
29 Burwood Park Road
Walton-on-Thames
Surrey KT12 5LH

British Wheel of Yoga
Grafton Grange
York TO5 9OP

Alcoholics Anonymous
PO Box 514
11 Redcliffe Gardens
London SW10

Migraine Trust
45 Great Ormond Street
London WC1N 3AY

British Migraine Association
178A High Road
Byfleet
Weybridge
Surrey

National Association for Pre-
Menstrual Syndrome
33 Pilgrim's Way West
Otford
Sevenoaks
Kent

Society of Homoeopaths
47 Canada Grove
Bognor Regis
West Sussex PO21 1OW

Council for Acupuncture
(umbrella group for the main
colleges)
Suite One
191A Cavendish Squre
London W1M 9AD

General Council and Register
of Osteopaths
21 Suffolk Street
London SW1Y 4HG

National Institute of Medical
Herbalists
41 Hatherley Road
Winchester
Hampshire SO22 6RR

MGI PRIME HEALTH
Private Medical Insurance
Prime House
Barnett Wood Lane
Leatherhead
Surrey KT22 7BS
0372 386060